THE KINGS OF EL DORADO

THE KINGS OF EL DORADO

by

Thomas Dickey, John Man,
and Henry Wiencek

Treasures of the World was created by
Tree Communications, Inc.
and published by Stonehenge Press Inc.

TREE COMMUNICATIONS, INC.

PRESIDENT
Rodney Friedman

PUBLISHER
Bruce Michel

VICE PRESIDENTS
Ronald Gross
Paul Levin

EDITOR
Charles L. Mee, Jr.

EXECUTIVE EDITOR
Shirley Tomkievicz

ART DIRECTOR
Sara Burris

PICTURE EDITOR
Mary Zuazua Jenkins

TEXT EDITOR
Henry Wiencek

ASSOCIATE EDITORS
Thomas Dickey   Vance Muse   Artelia Court

ASSISTANT ART DIRECTOR
Carole Muller

ASSISTANT PICTURE EDITORS
Deborah Bull   Carol Gaskin
Charlie Holland   Sabra Moore
Linda Silvestri Sykes

COPY EDITOR
Fredrica A. Harvey

ASSISTANT COPY EDITOR
Cynthia Lingo

PRODUCTION MANAGER
Peter Sparber

EDITORIAL ASSISTANTS
Carol Epstein   Martha Tippin
Holly McLennan Wheelwright

FOREIGN RESEARCHERS
Rosemary Burgis (London) Bianca Spantigati Gabbrielli (Rome)
Patricia Hanna (Madrid) Alice Jugie (Paris)
Traudl Lessing (Vienna) Dee Pattee (Munich)
Brigitte Rückriegel (Bonn) Simonetta Toraldo (Rome)

CONSULTING EDITOR
Joseph J. Thorndike, Jr.

STONEHENGE PRESS INC.

PUBLISHER
John Canova

EDITOR
Ezra Bowen

DEPUTY EDITOR
Carolyn Tasker

ADMINISTRATIVE ASSISTANT
Elizabeth Noll

THE AUTHORS: Thomas Dickey, associate editor at Tree Communications, wrote
Chapter Five in this book. John Man wrote Chapter Three and is also author of
The Day of the Dinosaur, The Waorani and two novels. Henry Wiencek, text editor
at Tree Communications, wrote the remaining three chapters of this book.

CONSULTANT FOR THIS BOOK: Julie Jones, whose specialty is pre-Columbian art, is
the curator of the department of Primitive Art at the Metropolitan Museum of
Art in New York City.

COVER: *One of a pair, this large gold ear ornament from southern Colombia may have belonged to a chief. Of hammered gold embossed with a human face and intricate, beadlike patterns, the piece was crafted between the ninth and thirteenth centuries* A.D.

TITLE PAGE: *Painted with the red pigment cinnabar and adorned with copper appliqués on the ears and under the nose, this gold mask lay on the face of a mummified Chimú noble. Exceptionally skilled as goldworkers, the Chimú of Peru flourished from the tenth century until about 1470, when the empire-building Incas overwhelmed them.*

OVERLEAF: *This fragment of painted cloth, once possibly a Chimú wall hanging, bears an image that consistently recurs in ancient Peru: the human figure. This one holds a staff and stands under an arching serpent, which undoubtedly represents the heavens.*

ABOVE: *Slightly more than nine inches tall, this silver llama wears a saddle blanket of brilliant crimson. One of the Incas' few domestic animals, the llama was a fitting emblem of prosperity, and effigies like this one often served as offerings in holy places.*

CONTENTS

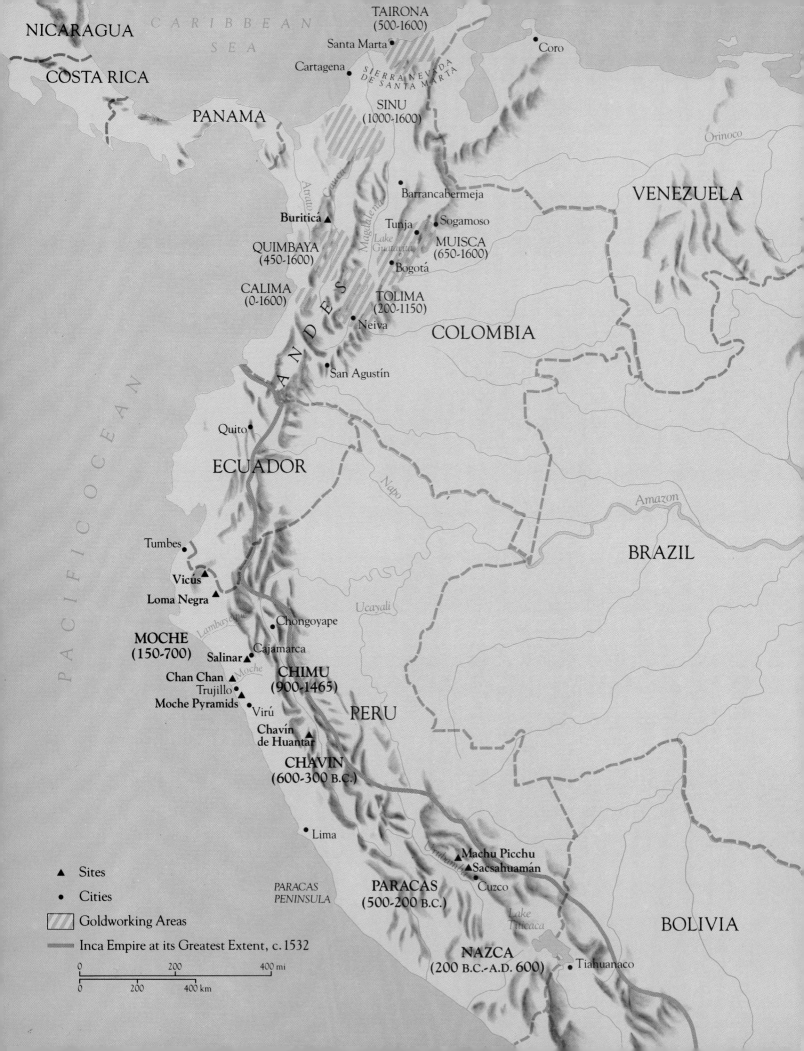

NICARAGUA

COSTA RICA

PANAMA

CARIBBEAN SEA

TAIRONA
(500–1600)

Santa Marta

Coro

Cartagena

SIERRA NEVADA DE SANTA MARTA

SINU
(1000–1600)

VENEZUELA

Orinoco

Barrancabermeja

Buriticá ▲

Tunja

Sogamoso

QUIMBAYA
(450–1600)

MUISCA
(650–1600)

Lake Guatavita

Bogotá

Magdalena

CALIMA
(0–1600)

TOLIMA
(200–1150)

A N D E S

Neiva

COLOMBIA

San Agustín

Quito

ECUADOR

Napo

Amazon

BRAZIL

Tumbes

Vicus ▲

Loma Negra ▲

Lambayeque

Chongoyape

Ucayali

MOCHE
(150–700)

Salinar ▲

Cajamarca

Moche

Chan Chan ▲

CHIMU
(900–1465)

Trujillo

Moche Pyramids ▲

Virú

Chavín
de Huantar ▲

PERU

CHAVIN
(600–300 B.C.)

PACIFIC OCEAN

Lima

Machu Picchu ▲
Sacsahuamán ▲

▲ Sites

• Cities

Goldworking Areas

Inca Empire at its Greatest Extent, c. 1532

Cuzco

PARACAS
PENINSULA

PARACAS
(500–200 B.C.)

Lake Titicaca

BOLIVIA

0   200   400 mi

0   200   400 km

NAZCA
(200 B.C.–A.D. 600)

Tiahuanaco

THE LANDS OF EL DORADO

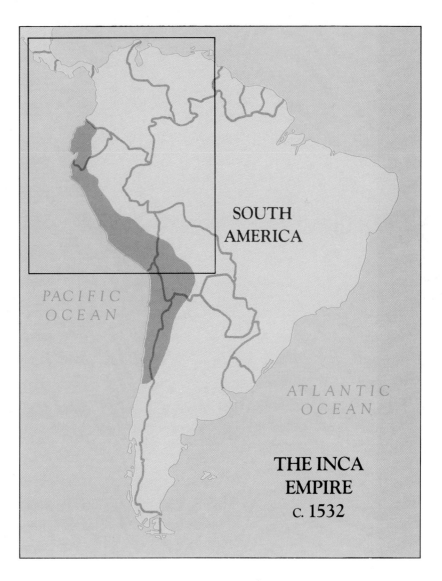

SOUTH AMERICA

PACIFIC OCEAN

ATLANTIC OCEAN

THE INCA EMPIRE c. 1532

In the northwest region of South America lies some of the world's roughest landscape: a virtually rainless desert on the coast and inhospitable mountain peaks inland. Yet this was the homeland of brilliant Indian cultures. On the map opposite, with modern boundaries drawn in for reference, are the civilizations that flourished in ancient Colombia and Peru, with their approximate dates. Within the six striped regions in Colombia, the Indians fashioned objects of gold for many centuries. In all but one of these areas, gold-working came to a halt about 1600, by which time the Spanish conquistadors had eradicated many tribes and extinguished their cultures. The Spaniards, and many other Europeans, had been lured in large numbers to South America by the hope of finding El Dorado, "the Gilded Man"—a king said to cover himself entirely in gold dust for his coronation. In time, "El Dorado" came to mean an entire kingdom of fabulous wealth, for which explorers vainly searched in what is now Colombia.

Farther south, in Peru, the Spaniards discovered the realm of the Incas, a two-thousand-mile-long domain, with its capital at Cuzco in the Andes. Before the Incas built their empire, Peru had seen the rise of several cultures. The names and dates of these civilizations are on the map.

I

THE CHAVIN CULT

LORDS OF THE JAGUAR

El Dorado—the words still evoke the image of treasure beyond counting, beyond imagining. Few legends have so profoundly captivated the minds of men, so inflamed their greed, and led so many believers to their deaths, as did the legend of El Dorado in the sixteenth century. In the late 1530s Spanish conquistadors in South America heard from the Indians there of a king entirely covered in gold dust, who tossed heaps of gold and emeralds into a lake as offerings to his god. The Spanish called this king El Dorado, "the Gilded Man."

The tale of El Dorado tantalized the Spanish and tempted Portuguese, Dutch, English, and Germans to South America. At that time gold was extremely scarce in Europe—so scarce that its value had soared by more than one thousand percent in just fifty years. Hundreds of gold-hungry adventurers flocked to South America and trekked thousands of miles through swamps, jungles, deserts, and mountains in search of the Gilded Man and his realm of gold.

To the European explorers, the story of El Dorado sounded

South America's peoples had already created high cultures, fine arts, and a farming technology when, about 100 B.C., a Peruvian potter made this painted mask.

This pot from Peru's northern coast takes the shape of one figure carrying another piggyback. The complacent rider in earplugs, necklace, and elaborate coiffure or headdress may be a noble or a priest. The squatting bearer has a garment textured with marks in the clay to resemble fur or hairy fiber.

perfectly credible, for they were finding that such marvels were commonplace in the New World. One Spanish explorer saw a king wearing "a gold helmet. . .and on his arms gold armbands. . .and on his chest and back many pieces of circular plates. . .and a belt of gold hung with gold bells." In Peru Francisco Pizarro discovered the fabulously wealthy Incas, who worshiped the sun in a temple with gold-plated walls and whose capital boasted a garden with trees, flowers, and animals of gold and silver. To the Incas, and to many other peoples of the New World, gold and silver expressed divinity and kingship. According to Incan legend, gold nuggets were "the sweat of the sun," and silver, "the tears of the moon," shed onto the earth at the beginning of time. The Incas worked these metals into images and ornaments that glorified the gods and the king. The European explorers took a more down-to-earth view: gold and silver equaled wealth, which was best expressed in ingots, easy to weigh and to count. Nearly every precious object the Europeans found, no matter how sacred or lovely, they melted down for bullion.

Scores of civilizations who fashioned golden treasures of exquisite beauty flourished in the northwestern regions of South America, lands of startling natural diversity. In Colombia, coastal plains, swamps, and low hills give way to the three chains of the northern Andes mountains, sometimes choked with vegetation, sometimes open and windswept. Two great rivers, the Magdalena and the Cauca, plunge down from the highlands, opening corridors to the Colombian interior. Farther south, in Peru, the towering mountain chains of the Andes cradle numerous grassy valleys, supporting llamas, guanacos, and vicuñas—three distant relatives of the camel. To the east of the Andes, the Amazon rain forest spreads away into an infinity of trees and rivers. In the west the coastal regions change dramatically, from equatorial mangrove swamps and rain forests in Ecuador to desert wastes in southern Peru.

These deserts are among the driest in the world. Protected inland from Amazonian downpours by the Andes, they are flanked to the west by the chilly Humboldt Current welling up from the depths of the Pacific. The current brings nutrients to the surface, creating rich fishing grounds, but it also prevents rain from reaching the coast. In some areas no rain has ever been recorded; but the coast is not totally barren. More than fifty rivers tumble down from the Andes across the desert, forming oases of greenery in the gray-brown wastes.

About twelve thousand years ago, tribes of nomadic hunters wandered into these lands from the isthmus of Panama. Over a period of thousands of years, the nomads developed a more settled way of life along the coast and in the cool mountain valleys. They dried mud in the sun and cut it into bricks to build houses with roofs of thatch. They cultivated maize in irrigated fields, trained the llama as a beast of burden, and rowed into the coastal waters on rafts of straw to catch fish.

Some time about 600 B.C., the far-flung settlements of the mountain valleys and the coast were knitted together by a potent force: religion. From unknown origins a cult sprang up, based on the ritual worship of a deity who was partly human and partly jaguar. The names of the cult and the jaguar-god have long been lost to history because the Andean peoples did not know how to write; but the religion has been named the Chavín cult, after the town near which the cult's chief temple was found.

The cult of the jaguar-deity spread rapidly through northern Peru, breaching the isolation of the mountain valleys and casting its influence over a distance of about 250 miles. Quite possibly the cult spawned a powerful aristocracy of priests and nobles, who may have grown rich from offerings brought to the deity's temple by believers. There is no evidence that the guardians of the cult imposed their beliefs on the people by military force. No defensive walls protected the main temple, and the leaders of the cult built no fortresses to guarantee the allegiance of the people. Apparently the three-century era of the Chavín cult was peaceful.

The adherents of the cult built their main temple on the banks of the Mosna River, in a valley over ten thousand feet above sea level. The temple was designed in a U shape, with forty-foot-high walls embracing a broad plaza. Rows of grotesque human and animal heads, carved from stone, projected from the outer walls. Inside, the

The plump body of a mother holding her overgrown child gives volume to this pot. In coastal Peru mothers often purposely deformed the skulls of children, perhaps for cosmetic reasons. Probably tightly bound in infancy, the children's skulls grew to be unnaturally elongated and narrow.

A STONE HEAD

THE TEMPLE DAIS

THE SANCTUARY
OF THE JAGUAR

In a treeless valley on the western side of the Andes, where several ancient trails meet, stands the temple compound of Chavín de Huantar, perhaps the primary ceremonial center of the cult of the Chavín. The cult might have arisen as early as 900 B.C. and dominated northern Peru for six centuries, coincident with a surge of growth in agriculture, prosperity, and trade. Farmers and fisherfolk, hoping to ensure the earth's fertility, probably flocked to the stone temples of Chavín de Huantar to worship their jaguar- and reptilelike gods. Gathered in the compound's sunken plazas, these pilgrims would have observed rites performed on the great temple's raised platform (above, right). The black and white stones of its lintel may have symbolized the fertile male and female forces in nature. Seemingly, only priests used the passageways and rooms (above, left) inside the platforms and temples where stone effigies of the gods glowered in darkness.

The rubbing opposite from a flat-carved stone reveals the image of a god. In each clawed hand he holds an ornate staff. His grimacing lips bare a jaguar's fangs. And rising from his head is a crownlike apparatus curling with snakes.

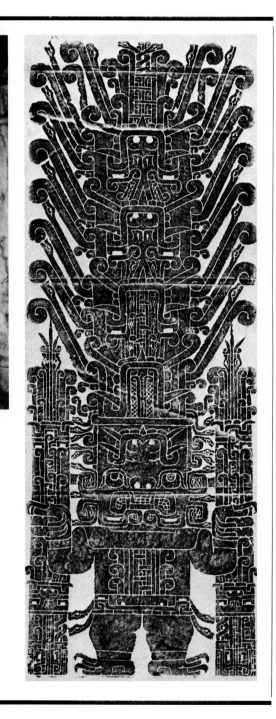

builders constructed a bewildering maze with rooms and passageways on three levels. At the crossing of two passageways, priests erected the image of their god—an idol fifteen feet high of a man with the head of a jaguar. The mouth curls into a snarl; a tusk juts out over the lower lip; the hands and feet end in claws. Mysterious and awe inspiring, the image was, and remains, a commanding presence in its sanctum, a small chamber where only the priestly elite was admitted. A narrow tube connects the jaguar's chamber with a passageway above, and it is possible that sounds carried through this tube reverberated in the chamber, like guttural pronouncements of the fierce god.

The rituals that took place in the presence of the idol are not known, but a carving in a courtyard of the temple provides a clue. The carving shows a man, perhaps a deity or priest, clutching stalks of the San Pedro cactus, a plant that produces the powerful hallucinogenic drug, mescaline. For centuries the inhabitants of the Andes have boiled pieces of the San Pedro cactus to produce a liquor rich in mescaline, which they drank or poured down their nostrils. Perhaps the priests of the jaguar, after ritually consuming the liquor of the cactus, entered the deity's chamber and interpreted the oracular utterances of the jaguar.

From coastal fishing villages and from highland farms, believers made pilgrimages to the Chavín temple. Possibly they venerated the jaguar as a "king of beasts" who symbolized the vital force of nature and controlled the fertility of fields, waters, and forests. Before the people could hunt or fish, priests may have sought the jaguar's consent through rituals and sacrifices.

Wherever the Chavín cult took root, believers fashioned stone carvings of eerie complexity, inspired by the idol of the jaguar-god and the decorations on the walls of the Chavín temple. Chavín artists carved gods, men, and animals using a visual code: sometimes a leg was represented by a tongue or a spine by a row of teeth. Around these symbolic mouths and teeth, the artists carved small faces, with the result that Chavín carvings were crowded with heads. Very often a mass of snakes represented hair. On monumental stone sculptures the writhing snakes and the profusion of heads were a nightmarish and daunting symbol of the jaguar-god's power. When the people of the Andes learned to work gold, the fierce imagery of the Chavín cult shone on the crowns and breastplates of the rulers.

The people of the Andes were among the first in the New World to use gold, starting about 400 B.C. The mountains around them were rich in gold, in the form of tiny nuggets washed out of volcanic rock by rain. The nuggets tumbled down mountain streams and settled at calm spots, where the Indians retrieved them by sifting the silt of the stream bed. Goldsmiths heated the nuggets on hot charcoal and fused them into larger pieces, which they hammered into sheets. Gold becomes brittle after it has been hammered too much, but the Chavín goldsmiths were able to solve this problem. Perhaps by accident the goldsmiths found that brittle gold can be softened by reheating it. They perfected the technique—known as annealing—of repeatedly hammering and heating a sheet of gold until it was thin enough to be wrought into delicate and complex designs.

Gold quickly became a badge of power and wealth. Not long after the Chavín culture first learned to work gold, a nobleman, perhaps the ruler of a tribe, was buried with three gold crowns, two of which carried the image of the divine jaguar. This potentate, whose realm was near the modern town of Chongoyape, Peru, also wore a headband and ear ornaments of gold. Not far from this grave, another nobleman and two women were buried with a small trove of gold—beads, rings, and delicate golden seashells.

One type of Chavín object that doubled as an ornament and as a usable implement was the gold spoon. Spoons unearthed in Chavín graves have openings for a string, which might have attached the spoon to clothing or looped around the wearer's neck. The spoons have handles modeled in the shapes of animals or men, which made them attractive pieces of jewelry. But a nobleman would have also kept such a spoon close at hand because it was a drug implement. Chavín nobles chewed the dried leaves of the coca plant, which contain the drug cocaine. As he chewed the leaves, the nobleman put into his mouth a small amount of powdered lime, a substance

A man, about seven inches tall and holding pan-pipes, and two tiny women probably went with a corpse to its grave to provide companionship in the afterlife. The ceramic sculptures bear traces of reddish cinnabar, an ore of mercury that was sometimes dusted on the dead.

derived from crushed seashells, which hastened the effect of the cocaine in the leaves. Chewing coca leaves was a privilege reserved for the most part for males of the nobility, who measured out the necessary powdered lime with their gold spoons. Coca leaves probably stimulated a mild euphoria in the users, who may have chewed the leaves at religious rites. In all likelihood Chavín goldsmiths and sculptors found inspiration in coca leaves and other drug-producing plants. For example, a drug produced by an Andean vine can induce writhing, serpentlike visions that may have been the source of the Chavín obsession with snakes.

The priests and nobles of the Chavín cult gradually lost their hold on the Andes peoples. At some unknown time a new divine image was set up at the Chavín temple. Local religions asserted themselves in the valleys of the Andes, and the old cult of the jaguar-god began to fade in importance by 300 B.C. But it did not disappear completely: the jaguar-god, and his intimate link to the fertility of fields and waters, were too deeply rooted in the minds of the people to vanish utterly. For centuries the image of the fierce, divine jaguar haunted the imaginations of the Andes peoples.

The treasures of gold inspired by the Chavín cult also endured. Some time after the cult had lost its dominance in the Andes, a wealthy nobleman or priest buried a cache of gold on a hilltop near the modern town of Huarmey, in western central Peru. Probably he was hiding the gold during a war and never returned to reclaim it. He buried a few objects of gold made in his own era, but mostly he buried Chavín gold: a pair of delicate vessels, ten discs of gold, and three headdresses, which mimicked in gold the appearance of feathered plumes. Obviously the Chavín pieces were the man's treasured heirlooms, prized not only for their beauty but also as tokens of an earlier time when peace reigned under the aegis of the jaguar-god, and men did not have to bury their treasures.

When the Chavín cult was still at its height, the worship of the jaguar-god spread south to one of the most desolate places in Peru, the Paracas Peninsula. Nothing grows in the rose-red sands of Paracas; even the hardiest flora of the desert cannot take root there

TEXT CONTINUED ON PAGE 22

An early Peruvian nobleman may have hung this five-inch, gold disc around his neck by a cord threaded through the two holes in its top. The hammered designs of a jaguar face in its center, and interlaced ribbons on its rim, have been heightened by cinnabar rubbed into their crevices.

BADGES OF AUTHORITY

Among the first Americans to craft objects from gold were Peruvian followers of the Chavín cult who, about 400 B.C., washed the refuse from bowls of river silt and collected the heavy, precious nuggets that remained. Hammering these into flat sheet metal, they then fashioned a variety of ornaments and ceremonial utensils, doubtless for members of the noble class. Along with his ordinary loincloth and cap, the well-dressed nobleman might wear gold earplugs, necklace, headband, and—suspended from a neck cord—gold tweezers for beard plucking. On ceremonial occasions he might add a high gold crown and a tunic or cape sewn with gold plaques. His noble wife probably wore gold finger rings and strings of beads, fastening her mantle with a gold stickpin before admiring her image in a mirror of polished stone.

Nobles and goldsmiths alike were specialists newly created by Peru's first high civilization—a civilization founded on the cultivation of maize. Given a position of social authority, the nobleman could marshal his people to work hard for regular, bountiful harvests, and he may have interceded on their behalf with the gods. The goldsmith, cutting his glistening sheets into patterns and embossing them with symbolic designs, provided the nobleman with emblems of his special authority and high caste.

A little gold man, wearing ear ornaments, perched on a stool, and blowing a conch-shell trumpet, forms the hollow handle of this spoon. The conch, a symbol of male authority, may have figured in the Chavín rituals, in which the participants used hallucinogenic snuff prepared with such a spoon. The man is made of sheet gold—beaten and soldered.

Possibly made to be sewn on a cloth garment, this gold plaque bears the fanged jaguar-man face wreathed in snakes that was common in Chavín temple stone carvings.

This jaguar plaque has a raised tail ending in a face with feline traits. Goldsmiths probably embossed all such designs with tools made of deer antler or bone.

This cylindrical gold crown, about nine inches tall, is embossed with the horned likeness of a major Chavín god. The mask of a glaring animal covers his chest as he stands, a staff clutched in either hand.

21

TEXT CONTINUED FROM PAGE 17

because the region is extremely arid. From 500 B.C. to 200 B.C., a tribe lived on this peninsula in underground houses of one or two rooms, walled with stones and reached by a tunnel or a stairway. Little is known about the way of life of the Paracas people, but a great deal is known about their way of death.

Early in their history the Paracas people buried their dead in underground vaults dug out of soft stone to a depth of about twenty feet. The vaults have the shape of bottles—narrow near the surface, where the stone is hard, and flaring out below. As many as fifty-five bodies were buried in one of these bottle graves, accompanied by funeral gifts that were usually modest. Later in their history, at a time that is not precisely known, the Paracas people became obsessed with death: the living began to spend much of their time preparing extravagant treasures to accompany the dead to the afterlife. These treasures were not gold or silver, but cloth—textiles of extraordinary beauty and size, made solely to shroud the bodies of the dead. In a group of stone buildings known as the Paracas Necropolis, the bodies of 429 people—many of them probably rulers and priests—were laid to rest. The bodies were piled up within the buildings, a sign not of neglect, but of deep respect for the dead. Because the bodies were not buried, the living were able to reach their ancestors and care for them for years, perhaps decades, after they had died.

All of the bodies were carefully mummified. Intestines, lungs, muscles, and the heart were removed. Sometimes the embalmers severed the head from the corpse and removed the brain. The body was smoked over a fire to preserve it, compressed into a tight ball, and bound. The embalmers placed the body in a basket and wrapped it first in a plain cotton sheet. Some of these sheets were immense. The largest one found in the necropolis measures about eighty feet by twenty feet. This single piece of cloth contains nearly two hundred miles of thread and certainly would have required teams of weavers to make.

After the body was wrapped in cotton, it was dressed in layer upon layer of richly embroidered clothing—shirts, skirts, ponchos, turbans, belts, and mantles, one over the other in increasing size until

BLIND FAITH

The Nazca people lived on Peru's south coast from about 200 B.C. until A.D. 600, and—perhaps as heirs of the high cultures of both the Chavín and the Paracas peoples—they carried forward a tradition of artistic and religious fervor. Seemingly a clannish people inclined to small enterprise, they painted wonderful birds and animals on pottery but raised no great masonry honoring their gods or governors. Instead they built an ingenious irrigation system to water their crops, and, on the bleak desert below their hillside villages, they built a series of troughlike earthworks that were another kind of monument.

By removing a top layer of dark stones to show the lighter soil beneath, the Nazca people marked the desert floor with about forty square miles of straight lines, spirals, rectangles, and animal drawings of astonishing scale and precision. All the figures probably had religious meaning. A few, pointing to where stars or the sun rose on certain dates, may have served the Nazca people as a calendar. The perfectly straight lines, some of which stretch for twenty miles with only tiny deviations, were probably paths connecting their clan shrines. And the vast and exquisite animals they made, including a monkey, a bird, a spider, and a killer whale, doubtless signified in their myths. The Nazca people could not view the completed figures, so great was the extent of each: a work of blind, but energetic, faith.

The outline of a spider, perhaps one of the poisonous kind used in Peru for religious divination, extends more than 140 feet over the Nazca desert. It can be seen in its entirety only from the air.

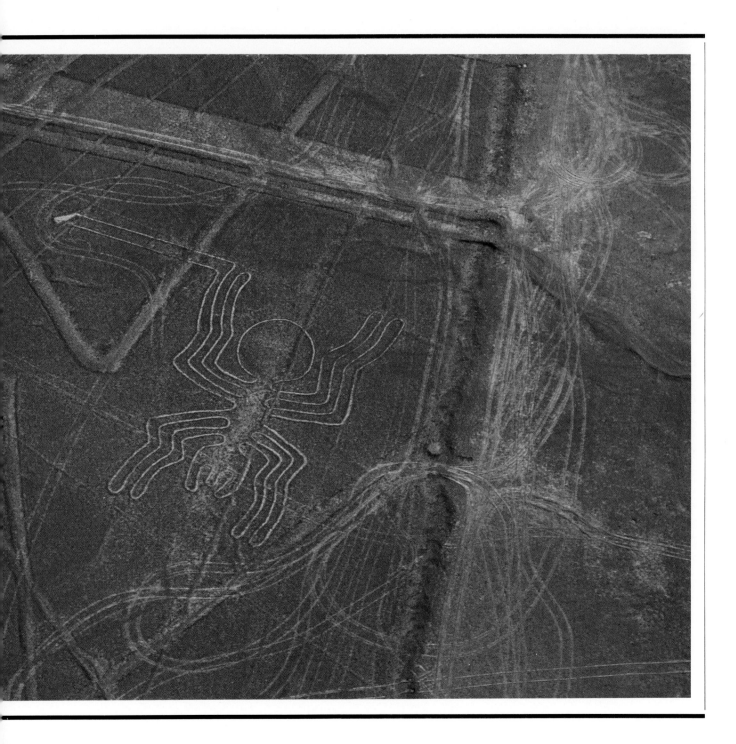

He in a flat cap and she with cropped hair, the man and woman of this ceramic figurine have separate heads, but bodies joined in a single column. Their facial decorations may declare them supernatural beings, even though some Peruvian mortals wore tattoos and body paint.

the outermost garments were large enough for a giant. One mummy was clothed in twenty ponchos and shirts, eleven mantles, and five belts. Tucked inside these layers of clothing was a variety of objects the man had used in his life: a dozen pieces of gold, a necklace of shells, a fan, a club, and a fox skin.

The funeral of a Paracas chief, so elaborately bedecked for the afterlife, was probably a surprisingly simple affair, judging by accounts of later Peruvian funerals. A European chronicler observed that the mourners expressed their regret at the chief's death with great emotion, but without pomp. "When a chief died the principal people of the valley assembled, and made great lamentations.... They had, and still have, the custom of mourning for the dead before the body is placed in the tomb, during four, five, or six days, or ten, according to the importance of the deceased, for the greater the lord the more honor do they show him, lamenting with much sighing and groaning, and playing sad music. They also repeat all that the dead man had done while living, in their songs; and if he was valiant they recount his deeds in the midst of their lamentations."

At such funerals the Paracas people burned some pieces of fabric. More than gold, fabric was a symbol of wealth to them. Wool, woven from alpaca hairs, had to be imported from the mountains at great expense. Dyes had to be laboriously mixed from plants, insect shells, and the excretions of shellfish. Often teams of weavers worked for months, even years, to weave and embroider a single funeral garment. Thus the number of clothes lavished on the dead of Paracas is astounding. But the clothing is even more remarkable for its supreme artistry. Vivid portraits of warriors, dancers, deities, and strange mythological creatures were embroidered on the clothes, and the arid sands of Paracas have preserved these exquisite shrouds for over two millennia. The meaning of the enigmatic pictures and the names of the men so sumptuously wrapped in them may never be known. But the shrouds themselves are testimony of the firm belief in immortality held by the Paracas people, who gave to eternity the greatest treasures they could make.

TAKING
FLIGHT

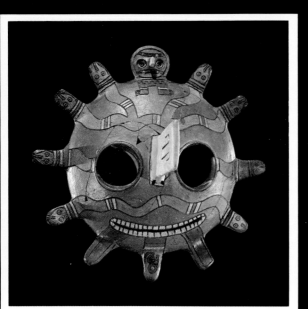

A pottery mask—crossed by snakes with protruding heads—decorated a mummy buried by the people of Paracas. It may be the visage of their ascendant, wide-eyed god.

Like other early Peruvians, the people of Paracas apparently considered cloth an important form of wealth. They seemed, as well, to insist on a certain code of dress, assigning each person a costume proper to his or her social station. From about 500 B.C. when they prospered—hunting heads for trophies and farming along the south coast—they devoted their superb weaving and embroidering skills to producing a dazzling treasury of wearable wealth, and then they buried it.

Hundreds of mantles, ponchos, headcloths, skirts, and other articles clothed Paracas's mummified nobility, whose interment had profound religious meaning. Spinners spun fine yarns, sometimes enriched by threads of the different colors taken from plant and animal substances. Weavers loomed each garment's basic cloth, often of locally grown cotton. But embroiderers preferred yarn of the wool of highland llamas and alpacas, acquired by trade, for it held dye well. Members of each noble's clan probably made the sumptuous garments and may have worked for years to complete a mantle sewn with about two million perfect, tiny stitches in over twenty shades. But the effort was worth it—the complex religious figures covering the garments probably acted as pictorial prayers, recording the nobles' kinship to the gods and speeding their souls into immortality.

This weaving, from a fringed poncho with a slit in the middle for the wearer's head, is of black cotton cloth worked in red, black, and yellow yarns. Large and small cats, perhaps local adaptations of Peru's fierce jaguar-god, are stitched in the geometrical style Paracas artists used when they began embroidery.

27

Multicolored woven squares make up the center of an eight-foot mantle with a border of embroidered beings. Each figure carries a staff

and wears an upside-down head with four antennalike streamers suggesting its mythical status. At the tip of each streamer is a tiny head.

A nocturnal bird akin to the whippoorwill—the nightjar—is embroidered at left in two color schemes on a fringed border. The whiskerlike appendages around the nightjar's beak are portrayed here tipped with coils, and from each bird's mouth comes a saw-toothed streamer, ending in a mask. The nightjar, the fox, the condor, and the killer whale inhabited the fertile sea and coastland of southern Peru, and all came to be important symbols of the Paracas religion.

The god who in time came to dominate Paracas religion had wide, staring eyes and a grinning mouth. Seemingly this wide-eyed god took on the traits of other creatures at will, and in the red border opposite he assumes the body of a bird. Small wide-eyed birds surround the big bird. As a convention of Paracas needlework, embroiderers would repeat one design many times on a single cloth, but they would vary the design's color, size, and details.

The length of mantle at right is embroidered with eighty-six versions of the same supernatural being, either god or demon, each on a yellow square. In the detail opposite, a thick, blue-edged streamer issues from the being's mouth. He has square, white eyes, and above them an orange, masklike forehead ornament topped by a turban trimmed with small black and white beans. Over the centuries the bean became common in Paracas embroideries, possibly as a metaphor for the trophy head taken in battle. The trophy head could have symbolized a rebirth of the spirit occurring when the body died. In the upper right hand corner of the design, a figure falls backward gripping a trophy head in each hand.

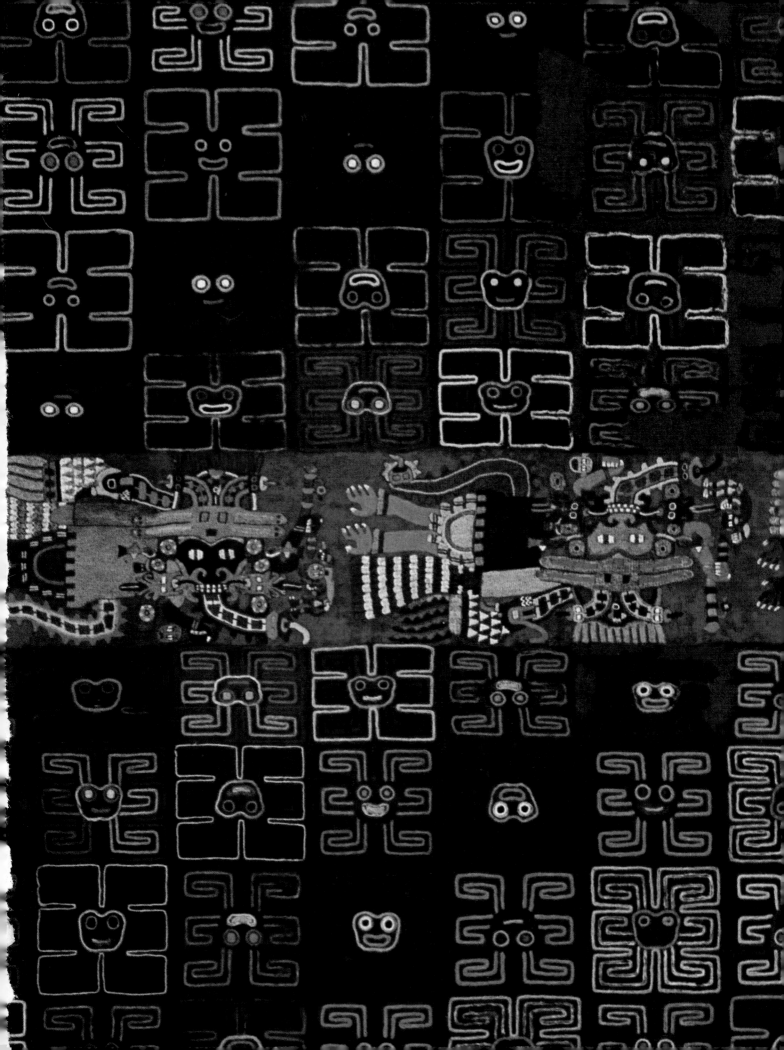

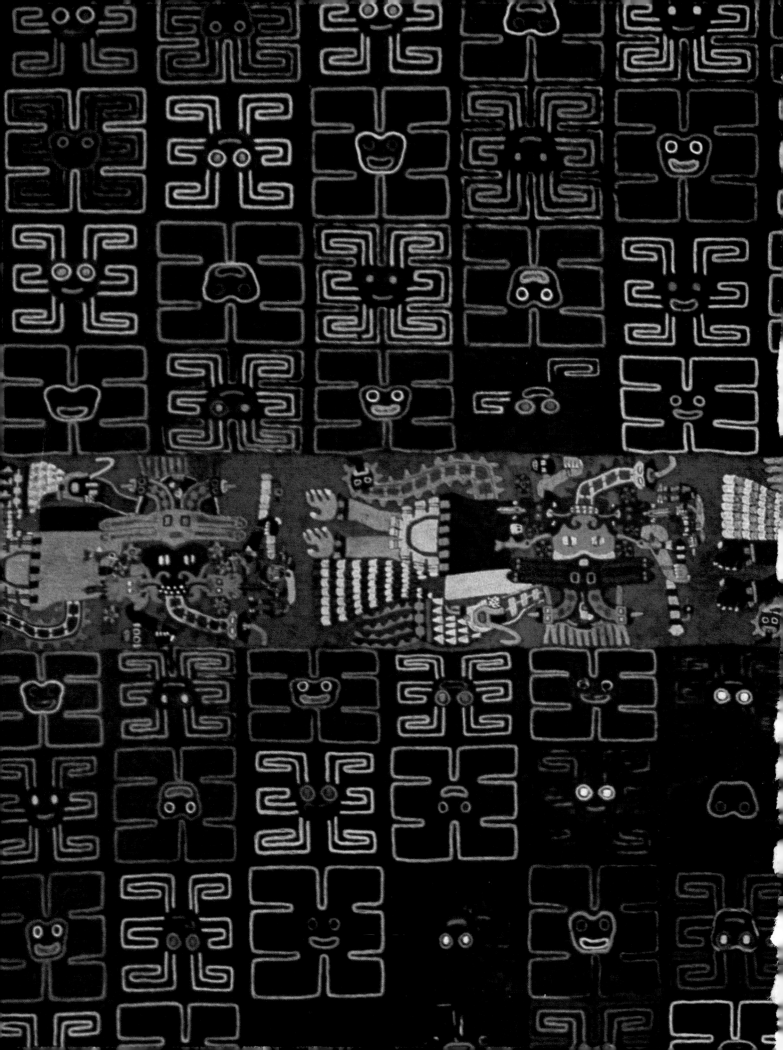

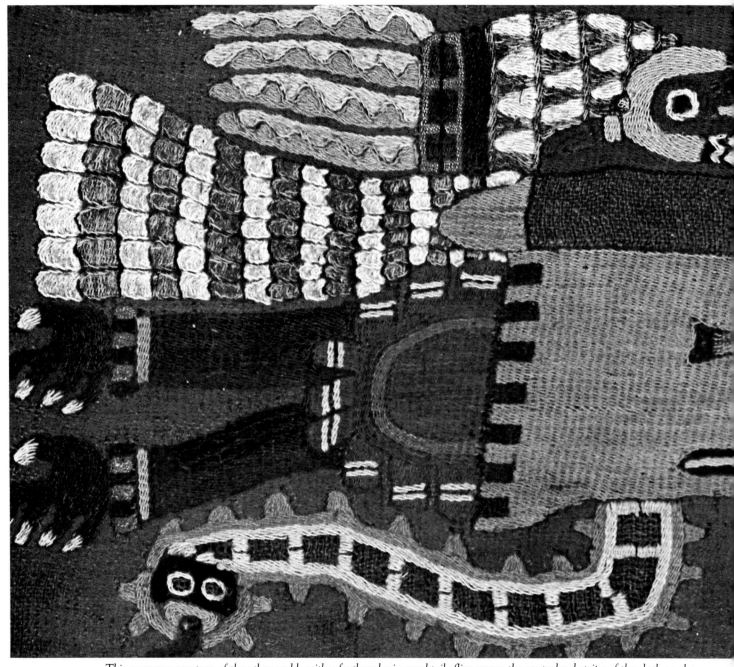

This awesome creature of the otherworld, with a feathered wing and tail, flies across the central red stripe of the cloth on the

FOLDOUT: *Rows of stylized faces framed in rectangles are embroidered on a black cloth and traversed by a procession of flying creatures stitched on red. As the sophistication of Paracas religion grew, its symbols became tremendously intricate, and embroiderers began to use colors in conventional and symbolic ways—white for toenails and fingernails, and black and white for eyes, became standard, as in these flying creatures. Rhythmic modulations of color, like the diagonal bands of framed faces, may have symbolized the phases of the moon.* ⟶

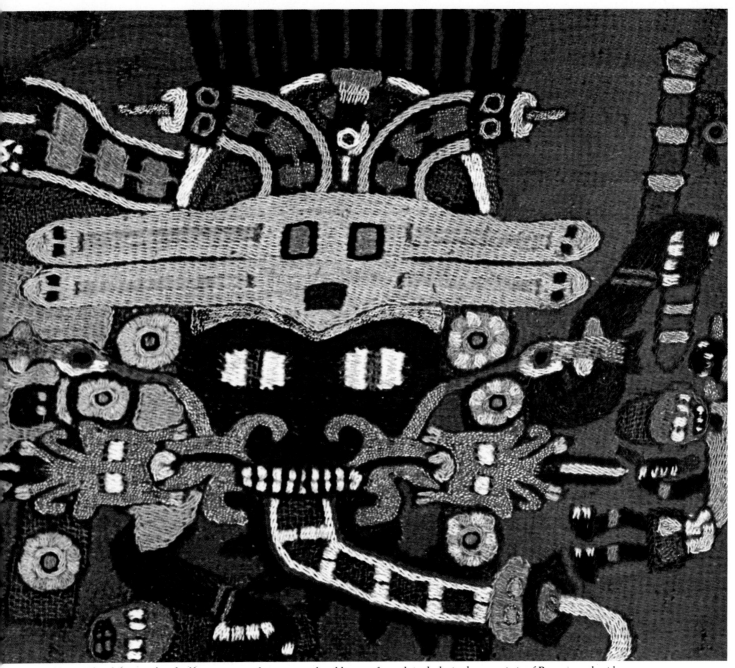

foldout. The elaborate detail of his costume, from ornate headdress to fancy loincloth, is characteristic of Paracas embroidery.

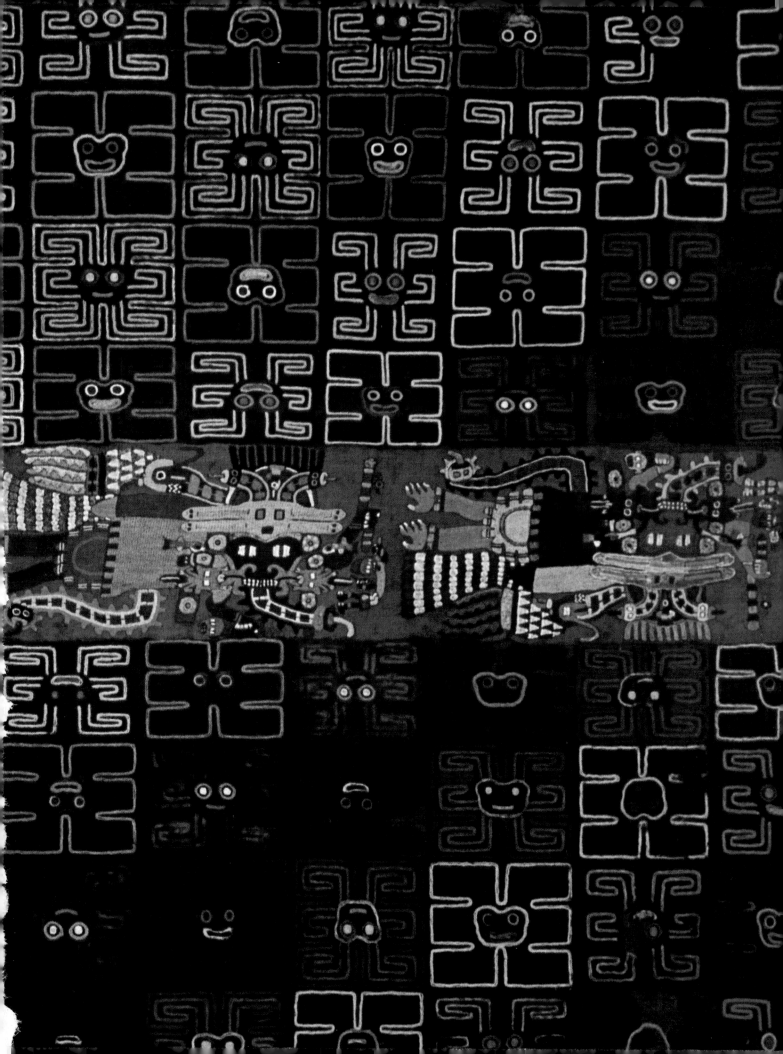

The stance and tunic, decorated with trophy heads, of this Paracas man resemble those of his companion in embroidery at right above. The different patterns of men's flowing headcloths and face paint may show their membership in separate clans or priesthoods.

Clasping a trophy head with a trailing topknot, this figure lacks streamers and the other tokens of divinity and thus probably represents a man of Paracas in ceremonial costume and face paint. Embroiderers often gave feet too few toes, as at left above.

As two foxlike creatures perch on his shoulders, and snakes with flickering tongues wreathe his head in a streamer, the mythical creature opposite grasps a pair of crossed staffs in each hand.

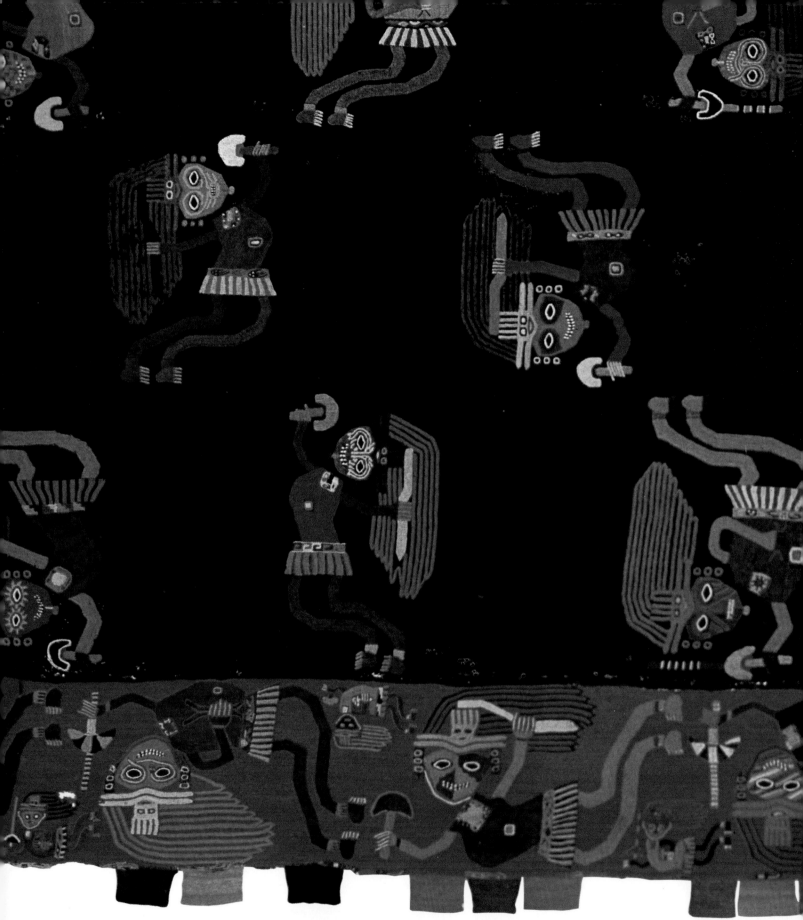

Flying men, each with a headdress streaming and wielding a short staff in one hand and a fan in the other—perhaps as badges of priestly authority—dot a dark mantle. The flying pose was associated with the wide-eyed god and may have derived from rites with hallucinogens.

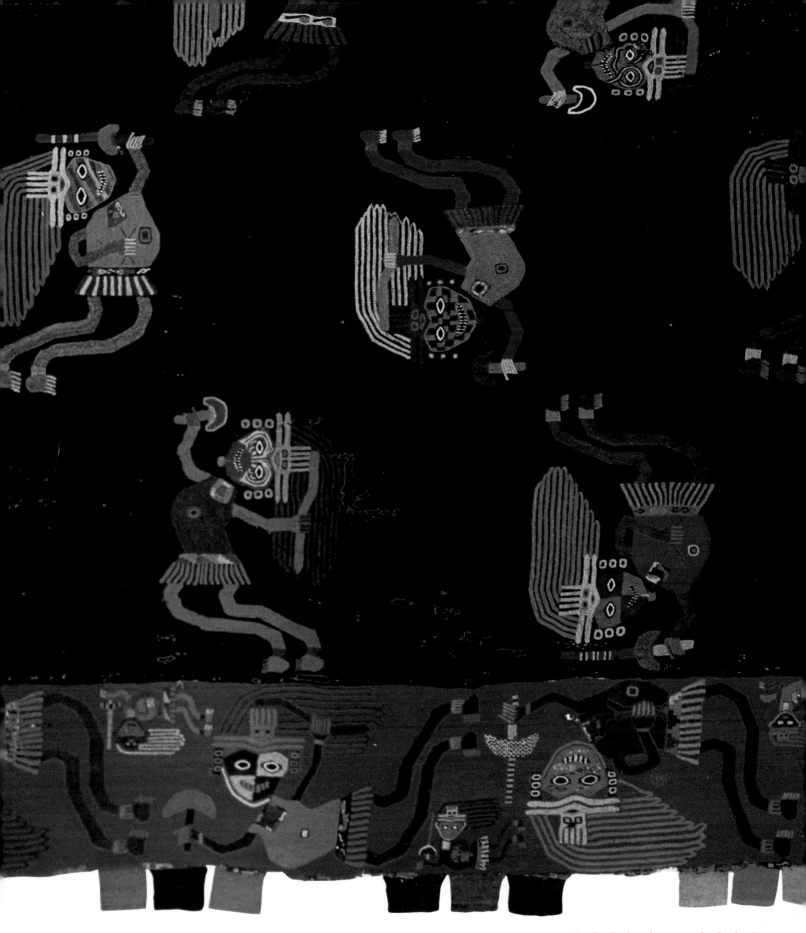

OVERLEAF: *By the feathered cape on his back, the cheerful figure repeated here may show his membership in a religious fraternity that had a falcon or condor for its emblem. His crooked staff, perhaps a ceremonial implement, seems to be hung with bells.*

II

THE MOCHE

KINGS OF THE HILLS

A long, low, mournful sound—the blast of a conch-shell trumpet—heralded the arrival of the king of the Moche, returning to his palace after a military campaign. Wearing the conical helmet of a soldier, the king was borne in an open litter by two attendants, accompanied by scores of mace-wielding bodyguards. The star-shaped heads on the maces of the guards marked them as the elite of Moche fighting men. A retinue of forty officials, responsible for the lord's personal comfort, followed the litter. Among these royal retainers marched the steward of the face paint, the keeper of the feathered robes, the master of the bath, and the royal cellarer, who was charged with maintaining an ample supply of maize beer.

The procession marched across the sandy floor of a valley dotted with small houses of adobe, to a pair of immense pyramids. The king's litter bearers cast a weary eye at the ramp that ran up the side of the taller pyramid and began the 250-foot ascent to the top. When the procession gained the broad top of the pyramid, one of the king's

This mask of corroded silver, sporting an ear ornament, once adorned the wrappings of a mummified Moche noble. One cheek is distended by a wad of coca leaves.

With an enormous lime gourd in front of him and a bag of coca leaves on his arm, this god or priest turns his face skyward. If mixed with lime and then chewed, coca yields a mild narcotic, which Moche men used in religious rites.

attendants, known as the preparer of the way, sprang forward to spread crushed seashells on the ground where the king would step as he climbed out of his litter and strode into his palace. His lofty residence towered over the Moche River and looked out toward the Pacific Ocean, just a few miles away. A few hundred yards across the valley stood a smaller pyramid, which supported the chief temple of the Moche. Below the feet of the king were the tombs of his predecessors, buried in vaults inside the pyramid along with hoards of gold—the accumulated wealth of a powerful military empire that flourished from 150 to 700.

The two pyramids, known in modern times as the Temple of the Sun and the Temple of the Moon, formed the capital of the Moche people, who conquered the farming settlements along the northern coast of Peru for a distance of two hundred miles. This strip of coast consisted largely of desert, penetrated by about ten rivers that were fed by rainfall in the Andes. The rivers held the key to survival in the desert, and the Moche cannily seized, one after the other, the regions at the edge of the Andes where the rivers entered the coastal plain. The Moche were highly skilled engineers, quite capable of diverting a river if it served their military purposes. Thus they could have held entire populations hostage with the threat of cutting off the water supply that brought life to the dry plains.

Once the Moche had conquered a region, however, they bestowed an abundance of water on their new subjects. The Moche conscripted gangs of laborers to erect irrigation works using the only material readily available along the coast—dirt. With enormous collective effort and ingenuity, the Moche and their subjects constructed an astonishing system of canals out of dried mud. One canal, eight feet wide and six feet deep, stretched for almost ninety miles. Another began in the Andes at an elevation of four thousand feet and carried water for seventy miles down to the coast. When valleys blocked the path of a planned canal, the Moche bridged them with aqueducts. One of the aqueducts reached a height of fifty feet and extended nearly a mile. To construct this engineering triumph, Moche laborers had to move some two million tons of earth.

Through their gargantuan labors the Moche created a prosperous farming empire, with an elite of priests and nobles literally overseeing the labors of the farmers. The lords of the Moche realm dwelled in hilltop estates of several houses, with secluded courtyards and shady porches. The houses were designed to be breezy and cool: they faced the Pacific to catch the prevailing wind, and each had a long, narrow opening below the roof to admit air and allow smoke from the kitchen fire to escape. The exterior walls of the houses were painted with colorful murals. Inside, the walls were festooned with the ceremonial clothes of the noble occupant. Wicker baskets or wooden chests held their jewelry. The houses at the top of the hill were surrounded by a wall, below which stood the huts of the noble's servants. Around the hill stretched the fields of the lord's domain, always under his watchful eye.

The loftiest residence in the realm, the symbol of the soaring ambition of the Moche people, was the palace of the king atop the Temple of the Sun. More than 1,000 feet long, about 450 feet wide, and about 250 feet high, the pyramid was the largest brick structure ever built in the New World. Only portions of the royal pyramid and its companion, the Temple of the Moon, survive; but they remain the greatest proof of the vast power wielded by the lords of the Moche. For more than a century, the Moche kings required each village in the empire to supply a gang of laborers to make bricks out of mud and pieces of grass and to build a particular section of one of the pyramids. The Moche organized the work of their huge labor force with precision. In order to monitor the productivity of the laborers, the Moche supervisors ordered each gang to stamp the bricks it made with a distinctive mark.

The enormous pyramids, so imposing in their height and sheer bulk, were nothing less than man-made mountains. The Moche believed that mountains were sacred places, the homes of guardian spirits. Therefore, the Moche ruler, who dwelled in the aerie atop the great pyramid, inspired awe and allegiance in the people toiling below because he was unmistakably linked in their minds to those mountain-dwelling spirits.

A man in a boldly checkered costume holds a gourd and a long stick, with which he adds powdered lime to the quid of coca in his mouth. His outsized ear ornaments no doubt denote high caste.

In the halls of his lofty palace, the ruler of the Moche and his noble entourage undoubtedly lived at ease, feasting from time to time on the meat of deer—a food reserved for the aristocracy—and on the maize beer called chicha. Chicha, a milky white concoction, was made from kernels of maize that had been chewed briefly, spit out into jars, and left to sit for a few days. Enzymes in the saliva of the chewers caused the maize to ferment, creating a slightly alcoholic brew that was the drink of king and commoner alike.

The base of the pyramid was the scene of many different Moche rituals that may have been performed to ensure the fertility of the fields. In one rite the celebrants flung golden flowers into the air. These were thin pieces of gold, cut into a shape roughly resembling a daisy. The gold pieces were attached to strings that were wound around copper staffs. The players—for this rite may very well have been a form of sport—twirled the staffs until the strings unwound and the golden flowers fluttered through the air. As the king watched the proceedings from his throne, priests observed the flight of the flowers and may have made predictions for the future based on the movements of the flowers. At this ceremony the priests wore imposing headdresses with copper models of foxes' heads, coated with gold. The Moche probably saw a parallel between the cunning and resourcefulness of the fox and the supernatural powers of the priests, who could interpret omens and divine the future.

The nobles who attended the ceremony of the golden flowers came richly robed, wearing pendants and collars of gold decorated with gold spangles that danced in the sunlight. A noble might also have worn a necklace made from hundreds of turquoise beads or a necklace of hollow gold discs containing pellets that rattled as he walked. Broad silver pendants hung from their noses, and in their earlobes the nobles wore round ornaments of gold, colorfully inlaid with bits of turquoise, shell, and quartz.

The king dressed in ornate, ostentatious splendor, with a gold disc in his nose and a flamboyant crown. A plume of osprey feathers swayed at the back of the crown, and a foot-high sheet of gold was attached to the front. Embossed on the sheet was the round,

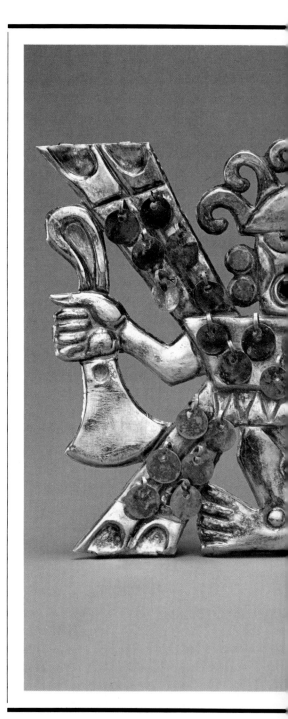

SEVERED HEADS

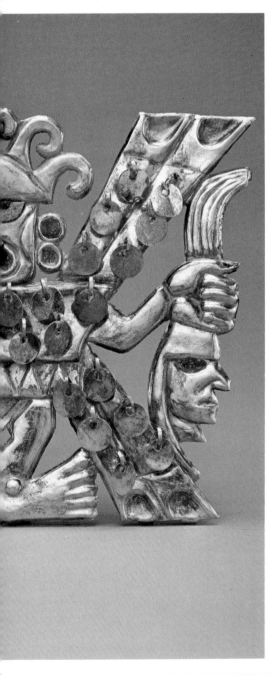

Perhaps because their physical surroundings were so harsh, the Moche believed in, and rigorously served, a harsh god. What his name and nature were may forever remain a puzzle: but he was fanged and feline in aspect and thus probably close kin to the jaguar, and he also had an appetite for human blood. The Moche often portrayed him, or his earthly representatives, drinking blood or accepting dismembered bodies as tribute. In particular he seems to have wanted heads, and Moche metalsmiths made a special kind of knife—the crescent-bladed *tumi*—for use in ritual decapitations. Mace heads and tumis were the only tools on which the Moche lavished metal, which they reserved instead for their spectacular jewelry.

The severed head is one of several themes that haunts Moche art. Heads appear in the hands of men and of deities, atop rattle poles and staffs, and on racks. Probably the Moche shrank the heads after they had acquired them. They may have believed that in the process they and their god somehow took on the courage and strength of their victims. Indeed the quest for these victims, rather than any desire for territory or power, might have driven warriors into battle and inspired them to fight well.

The miniature deity at the top of this sacrificial knife is fanged, like a feline, but two birds extend from his sides. The blade is of cast copper; the birds bear traces of inlaid shell.

The fanged being at left, in tunic and breechcloth and a cap with great golden curls, clutches a human head in one hand and a knife in the other. The bespangled rays might represent the sun, and the being might be the chief god of the Moche pantheon.

brooding face of a man, flanked by snarling doglike animals.

The Moche may have believed that their ruler was a divine being. A legend probably handed down from Moche times asserts that when a ruler was about to die he went into seclusion so that his vassals would not know that death had power over him. The king's closest associates buried him in secret and proclaimed that the king had sprouted wings and flown away. Another legend states that a dying king sealed himself in a vault so that no one would see him die, and his descendants would believe that he was an immortal. Though the Moche kings may have been buried in secret, they were nonetheless buried in splendor—entombed within their pyramid along with the golden treasures they had worn in life.

The names of the Moche rulers will probably never be known because the Moche left behind no written records. But they did leave behind a vivid pictorial record of their lives. The Moche were experts at molding and painting clay pottery, and their pots—some of which were probably fashioned by Moche priests—were among the most important treasures of their society. Many of the pots are portraits of the faces of rulers, about half life-size, possessing the unmistakable air of command. Moche noblemen were very often buried with these portraits of their king by their sides, as proof that they had been persons of high standing in life. Rulers were not the only subjects depicted on Moche pots. The potters molded and painted views of houses, battles, parades of prisoners, and religious ceremonies. Indeed the pots provide a rich lode of information about the Moche—the way they looked and the way they lived.

The pots reveal that the Moche were a short people, heavily built, with the round faces and high cheekbones typical of American natives. All the Moche men pierced their ears and noses to hold ornaments. The common man wore simple, painted wooden jewelry; but a lord of wealth sported gold ornaments, inlaid with shell or turquoise. The Moche painted their faces in a variety of ways that denoted status or occupation. Warriors, for example, colored the sides of their faces red or black, leaving a clear swath from the chin up to the forehead. Some warriors painted crosses on their faces,

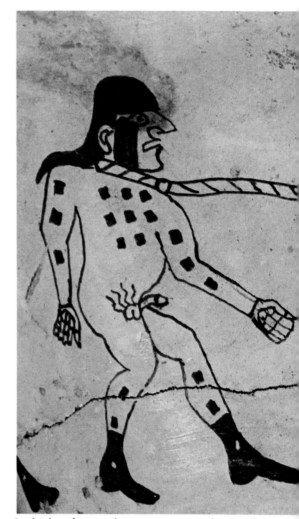

In this line drawing from a pottery vessel, a Moche warrior in a feathered headdress leads a captive at the end of a rope. Stripped naked except for his footgear—which may simply be body paint—the prisoner probably faced ceremonial decapitation.

others circled their eyes with black—emblems that may have stood for military ranks.

The prime weapon of the Moche warrior was the mace, with a thin shaft and a knob on the top. The Moche used this weapon with grim effectiveness, as shown in a battle scene on a pot where a warrior bashes an enemy's head, which splits open with a splash of blood. For fighting in tight quarters, the Moche mace was equipped with a sharp copper bayonet at the base. Not surprisingly the main armor worn by Moche warriors was a helmet—a sturdy protector of leather, wood, and copper, with a metal neckpiece and ear shields.

Chivalry was not one of the traits of the Moche warrior: he was a fierce, grim fighter who displayed no mercy to the defeated. Painted pots show prisoners bleeding from mutilated noses and victorious Moche warriors toying sadistically with their captives. They first stripped a prisoner to humiliate him and tied a short rope around his neck. Then the Moche warrior prodded his prisoner into running by jabbing him with the bayonet at the end of his mace. When the prisoner ran, the captor jerked on the rope, pulling the luckless man back onto the bayonet.

Cruelty ran deep in the Moche character. For example, they put a criminal to a slow and loathsome death: tied to a stake in the desert with a flap of skin cut out of his back to attract carnivorous birds, which devoured him piece by piece. Some Moche religious rites involved cannibalism, and a scene often depicted on Moche pots shows a ruler or god being presented with a goblet of human blood, drawn from the necks of bound and naked prisoners.

The religious beliefs of the Moche are not clearly understood, but the image of the jaguar—the deity of the old Chavín cult—often appeared on the walls of Moche temples. There is no evidence that the Chavín people performed human sacrifices, but the Moche apparently viewed the jaguar-deity as a voracious god that demanded human victims. Moche pots show men wearing fanged masks presiding over human sacrifices in the mountains. The victims, probably prisoners of war, were tossed from a peak onto the rocks far below.

Moche priests invoked the power of mountain spirits in the rituals

TEXT CONTINUED ON PAGE 58

Two figures, presumably men and both wearing face paint, dip their fingers into the bowls set before them and gravely sample the contents. Perhaps they are making chicha, a maize-based beer, which played a role in ceremonial occasions.

A woman, gazing upward, lies flat while a man examines or caresses her. His large earrings and elaborate, mushroom-shaped headdress mark him as a person of importance, probably a healer with magical powers and hence high caste in Moche society.

BEYOND THE
COMMONPLACE

Laboring without potter's wheels or any kind of technological advantage, Moche craftsmen stubbornly stuck to the most traditional of forms—the jug with a curved handle and spout. Yet over the centuries they modeled thousands of the most extraordinarily varied ceramics, unrivaled for their pictorial detail. The pots present what at first appears to be the whole spectrum of life. People eat, drink, embrace, wash their hair. Doctors heal, musicians pipe, women weave and give birth, warriors torment prisoners, hunters hunt. Men appear in vivid, sculptural portraits, chieftains as well as the sick and the blind. Oddly, though, the potters never intended these wares for cooking pots or domestic service, but ultimately as offerings for the graves of the mighty. Despite its richness, the pottery is as remarkable for what it omits as for what it shows. No one on any Moche pot tills the soil or cooks, washes clothing, or makes pottery—though ceramics must have been a major occupation. Couples make love, but never—as one modern authority points out—in any manner that could result in pregnancy. Women appear but seldom on the pots, and invariably in attitudes of joylessness. Indeed this world is prevailingly solemn. The faces are immobile; the eyes stare fixedly. Thus what seems to constitute a celebration of ordinary life may be, instead, ritualistic and mysterious: a record of occurrences outside the common run.

Leaning over a dish, a youth wrings the water out of his hair. Grooming and cutting the hair may have had ritual meaning. The Moche god was believed to wash his hair in the sea; and in combat a warrior pulled his opponent by the hair.

BLIND MAN WITH A DRUM

Disease and deformity were almost obsessive themes on the pots, especially eyelessness and other forms of mutilation, as at left and below, right. Possibly the Moche accorded special status to the handicapped. Bound captives, another favorite motif, were no doubt visible in large numbers on great ceremonial days, as were the chieftains. The captive below, left has his hands tied behind him. The grandee opposite wears nose and ear ornaments as well as body paint, with prominent knee spots, and a tunic with a pair of serpents on the chest.

CRIPPLE WITH A STAFF

PRISONER, SEATED AND BOUND

DIGNITARY WITH NOSEPLUG

TEXT CONTINUED FROM PAGE 53

In the procession above, rattle poles make a joyful noise. Craftsmen probably used shells to make the rattles, and they also fashioned ceramic panpipes, bugles, and whistles. The occasion here might be a military triumph, for atop each of the musical poles rides a severed head.

they performed to cure diseases, which the Moche probably believed were caused by evil spirits. As the sick person lay before him, the priest whistled and shook a rattle to attract friendly spirits and scare away the evil ones. He fed the patient herbs and a powder made from ground-up stones removed from the stomachs of sea lions. The priest himself drank a hallucinogenic liquor brewed from the San Pedro cactus. In the trance induced by the cactus, the priest was able to see evil spirits and tried to fight them off with a sword.

The Moche had little tolerance for a priest who failed to cure his patient. When a sick man died, the Moche tied his curer to the corpse with long ropes, buried the patient, and left the tethered priest lying on the ground over the grave.

The Moche empire endured for more than five centuries. Near the end of that time, the empire may have grown ever more rigid and oppressive. The pottery made by the Moche became more tightly stylized than before, suggesting that the ruling class may have demanded increasing conformity and subservience from the people. When a crisis arose in the seventh century, the empire's subjects, weary of an oppressive regime, may have refused to help defend it. Sometime in that century, invaders from an Andes civilization based around Lake Titicaca swarmed down from the mountains. The fierce warriors of the Moche were unable to stem the invasion. By about 800 the empire had collapsed, and Andean overlords installed themselves on the Temple of the Sun.

Early in the seventeenth century, long after the names of the Moche rulers and deeds of their warriors had been forgotten, the legend of the empire's wealth remained. Rumors that a fabulous treasure lay hidden in the Temple of the Sun attracted Spanish adventurers, who turned an old trick of the Moche against the bones of the Moche kings. The Spanish diverted the Moche River so that it washed against the pyramid, tearing away nearly two-thirds of it. More than six thousand pounds of gold treasures tumbled out of the tombs of the Moche kings, into the hands of the looters, and ultimately into the melting pot. At a stroke, the splendid, golden immortality, so yearned for by the Moche kings, was erased.

THE MAGIC BESTIARY

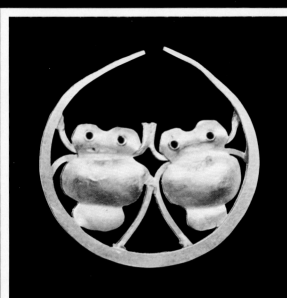

A pair of wide-eyed spiders adorns this gold nose ornament, which may have been crafted as early as the second century. Its diameter is only slightly more than an inch.

To the Moche nobles, gold and silver may have had some sacred or magical connotation. But whatever valuation the mighty attached to precious metals, the smiths who fashioned body ornaments of gold and silver were virtuosos of the art. They hammered gold and silver and often alloyed them with copper. They knew how to inlay, weld, solder, anneal, and use gold washes. Not only did they render the human face and form in metal, but also an astonishing menagerie of animals: jaguars, spiders, owls, snakes, hogs, and other beasts that may have had some magical significance. The Moche probably believed that certain men could change into animals and back again, and that certain animals possessed the power to heal. Perhaps for this reason Moche creatures often exhibit a puzzling ambiguity. A fox, for example, may resemble a snake, or a man will wear the head of a bird. The ornaments here and on the following pages might have belonged to priests and surely display the imagery of supernatural beliefs.

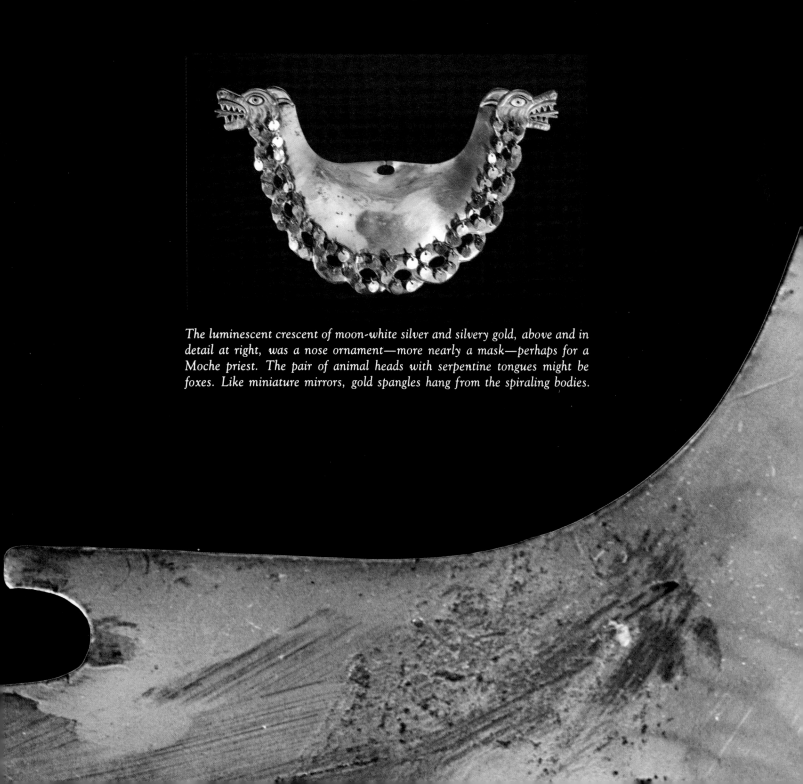

The luminescent crescent of moon-white silver and silvery gold, above and in detail at right, was a nose ornament—more nearly a mask—perhaps for a Moche priest. The pair of animal heads with serpentine tongues might be foxes. Like miniature mirrors, gold spangles hang from the spiraling bodies.

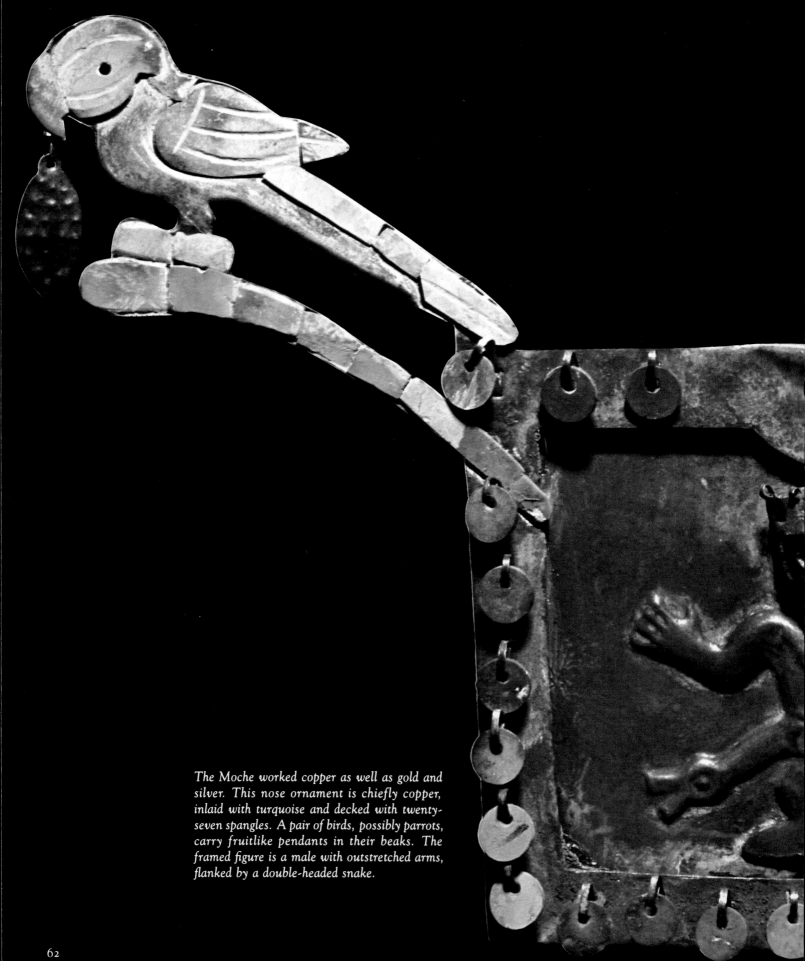

The Moche worked copper as well as gold and silver. This nose ornament is chiefly copper, inlaid with turquoise and decked with twenty-seven spangles. A pair of birds, possibly parrots, carry fruitlike pendants in their beaks. The framed figure is a male with outstretched arms, flanked by a double-headed snake.

OVERLEAF: *About two thousand years ago, an Andean goldsmith hammered and welded this intricate nose ornament, four and a half inches wide. Earlier and more delicate than most Moche work, it has a subject the Moche liked: spiders, here caught in a golden web. They are identical, with eight wispy legs.*

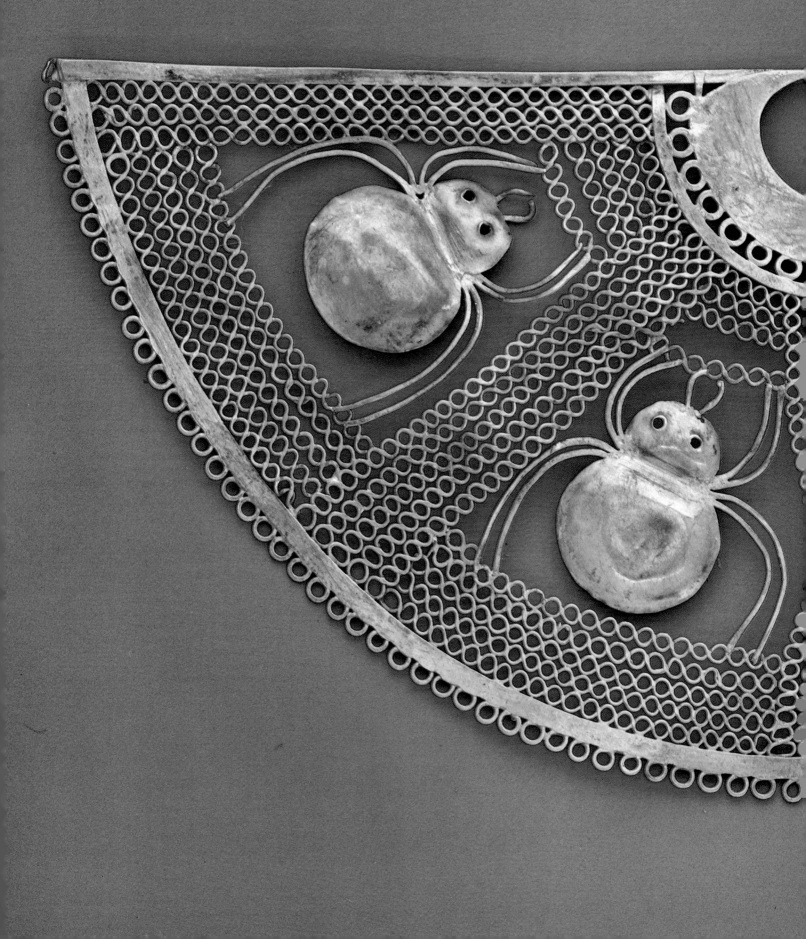

On the set of gold earplugs above, and in detail at right, a pair of warriors runs or dances. In one hand each clutches a spear or scepter and in the other hand a shield with a catlike head that resembles his own pale mask. In front of the shields, trophy heads dangle, supposedly as tokens of military prowess. Among the Moche, earplugs were often the object of infinite artistic care. The two circlets here are inlaid with turquoise, lapis lazuli, and other precious stones. Some sixty beads encircle the rows of filigree.

Winged figures with hawklike heads appear with mysterious frequency upon Moche ornaments, as on this pair of earplugs. The hurrying messengers, formed of a finely polished and fitted mosaic of turquoise and shell, could perhaps be actual couriers, garbed as birds—or demigods. In their outstretched fists they hold bags, the contents of which might be lima beans representing, both symbolically and literally, a good omen for future planting seasons.

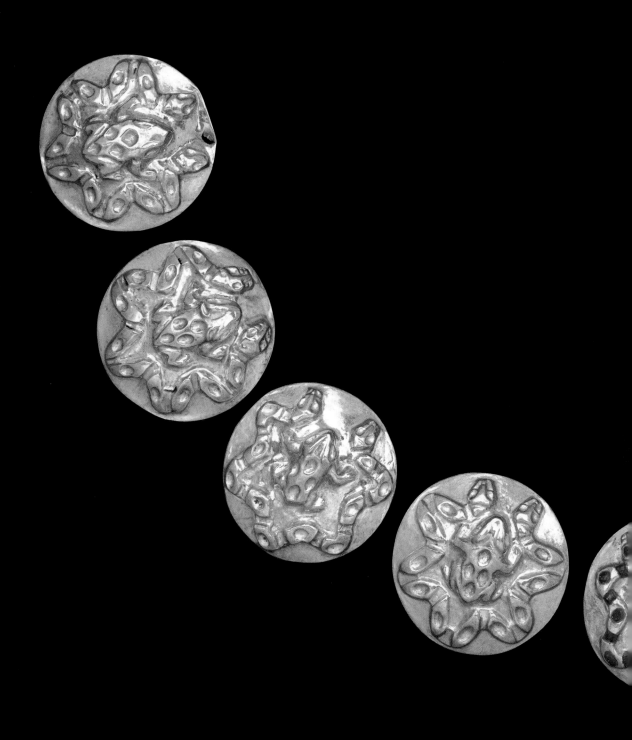

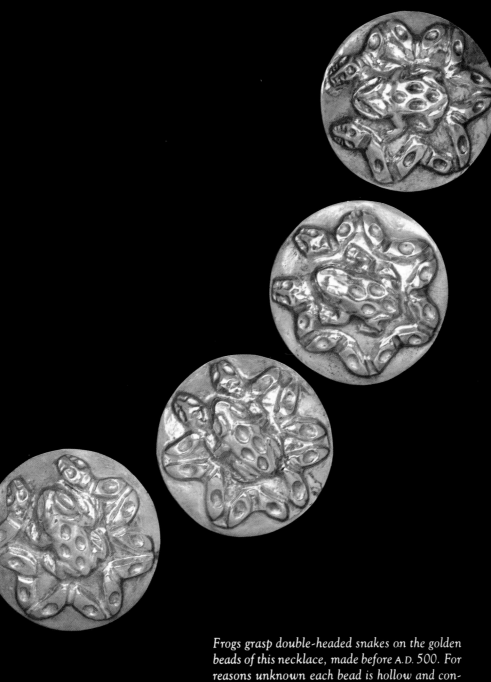

Frogs grasp double-headed snakes on the golden beads of this necklace, made before A.D. 500. For reasons unknown each bead is hollow and contains a pellet, perhaps so as to rattle as the wearer walked or danced. The serpent with two heads was a favored symbol in Peru.

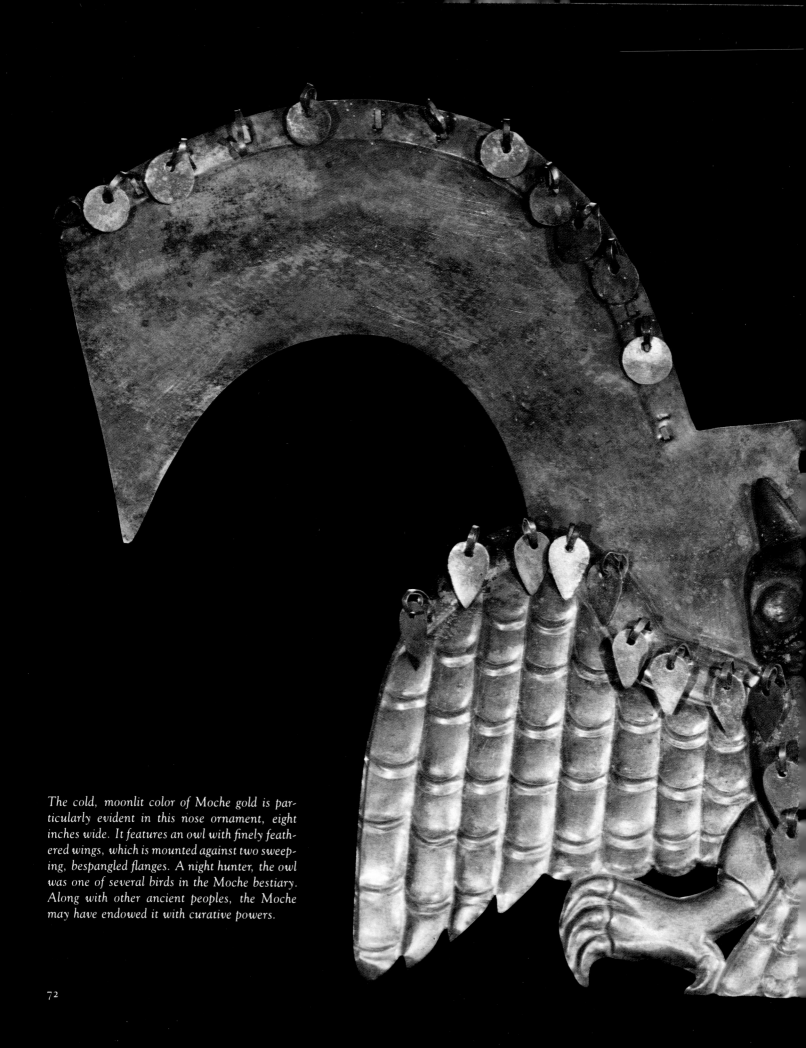

The cold, moonlit color of Moche gold is particularly evident in this nose ornament, eight inches wide. It features an owl with finely feathered wings, which is mounted against two sweeping, bespangled flanges. A night hunter, the owl was one of several birds in the Moche bestiary. Along with other ancient peoples, the Moche may have endowed it with curative powers.

III

ATAHUALPA THE INCA

SON OF THE SUN

Atahualpa, ruler of the Incas, king of the New World's greatest empire, son of the sun itself, was a decidedly unglamorous god-king. He was a thickset, muscular man with bloodshot eyes and a badly injured ear. Moreover, his position was far from secure—he was a usurper who had seized power from his brother in 1532 after a bloody civil war. He was careful, therefore, to emphasize his authority by employing all the trappings of majesty and divinity. He adopted a terrifyingly stern expression, often wore a cloak that covered his damaged ear, and surrounded himself with golden objects—symbols of the sun. His cups and plates were of gold. The litter on which he was carried was encrusted with gold, and his regalia included a set of golden earplugs as well as a headband decorated with gold.

He kept courtiers, generals, and civil servants at a distance, with a protective screen of beautiful servingwomen, whose tasks were many. They reverentially held the dishes from which he ate. They burned those objects he had used—his clothes, the rushes on his

In this sixteenth-century portrait Atahualpa, the last of the independent Incan emperors, adopts a regal stance that belies the shakiness of his far-flung empire.

Incan farmers, dressed up in gold earplugs for the planting festival, till the first soil of the season as their wives chant ritual songs. The woman at right is offering them the drink chicha, which was used in most public celebrations.

floor, his discarded food—to prevent lesser mortals from touching them. They even ate the hairs that fell from his head so as to avoid the risk of even such minor parts of his body falling into the hands of ill-wishers, who might use them to cast spells upon him.

With such rituals Atahualpa showed that he, the thirteenth "Inca"—a word that originally applied only to the king and was later adopted as the name of the whole tribe—was the fount of all civil, military, and religious authority. The rituals were also ways of conferring mystique on an empire that was still very young.

In the thirteenth and fourteenth centuries, the Incan rulers were no more than petty chiefs, squabbling with their neighbors over tiny tracts of land in the highland valley of Cuzco in the Andes mountains. The idea of expansion occurred first to the eighth Inca, Hatun Tupac, in the early fifteenth century. He grandly renamed himself Viracocha, "the Creator," and by the time of his death in 1438 had won a miniature empire, some fifty miles across.

Viracocha's son Pachacuti and grandson Topa built upon this small but secure foundation. Both leaders were dynamic and brilliant, and the territorial expansion they achieved was little short of miraculous. In just over fifty years, Pachacuti and Topa carved out an empire that, if it were outlined on a modern map, would stretch across parts of four nations: Ecuador, Peru, Bolivia, and Chile. By the time of Topa's death, in 1493, the Incan realm extended 2,750 miles from north to south, and from the Pacific coastal plains to the forested eastern slopes of the Andes mountains.

When establishing their desert-and-highland empire, the Incan rulers had been confronted with a fundamental problem: the lands were harsh, and the soil in some areas was poor. Most trees had long since been cut for fuel, and wild animals were few. Llamas, vicuñas, and guanacos provided wool, and llamas could carry loads of a hundred pounds; but there were no draft animals to haul very heavy loads or to help till the fields. Farming depended on human muscle. Men and women toiled their years away, weaving, raising guinea pigs for meat, and tilling the ground with sticks and foot plows to plant maize, squash, and potatoes—the rich food source native to the

Andes and unknown to the rest of the world until the sixteenth century. Life was nasty, brutish, and—in times of disease or harvest failure—short.

The emperors changed all that by imposing the rigid controls necessary to make life secure in a harsh land. On the coast the Incas organized the building of canals and sluices. They terraced the highlands, turning recalcitrant rock and precipitous slopes into fertile land. Farmlands and herds belonged to the state. Officials supervised the building of storehouses in cold, dry places to stockpile supplies such as dehydrated potatoes and dried meat, guaranteeing food both for state employees and for those in need.

In the Incan state there was little personal freedom for the common people: the empire was of a nature that demanded absolute conformity. Travel for personal reasons was forbidden. Officials often arranged marriages, pairing off the young people of local clans. Life was one of organized duties—building, clearing canals, mending terraces, digging fields, herding.

The empire was bound not just by firm administration but by superb communications as well. More than ten thousand miles of roads, as well as fords, viaducts, flights of steps, and swinging suspension bridges, linked the settlements of the empire. Along these highways teams of runners carried goods and oral messages— the Incas did not know how to write. They used a relay system, with each runner covering a short distance, then handing his package or repeating his message to a fresh runner at a way station. Messages and goods could travel up to 150 miles a day. Incas in the Cuzco valley, two hundred miles inland and eleven thousand feet up, could eat fresh fish caught a day or two before at the coast.

At the edge of the Cuzco valley stood the Incan capital, also called Cuzco. The city of Cuzco began to take shape in the fourteenth century under the sixth Inca, Roca. But it was the great conqueror Pachacuti who envisioned a grand capital, suitable for a mighty empire, in the fifteenth century. He drained swamps in the valley to make way for palaces and plazas. He also started the construction of a gargantuan fortress, called Sacsahuamán, on a

Farmers bring a large portion of their bi-annual maize harvest for storage in a government granary, above. Officials would distribute food to the needy or to villages where drought or famine had struck. Llamas, the pack animals on the right, were literally the backbone of Incan life.

The backrest of a brilliant Chimú litter, about two feet high by four feet wide, has paper-thin gold plates and imaginatively carved wooden figures. In Andean cultures it was the privilege of the ruler and his favorites to ride smoothly upon the shoulders of well-trained bearers, and the Incas enjoyed this custom as did the Chimú, whom they subjugated.

quayracapac

ynga ua ala conquista
de los cayanbis guancabi
ca caniari cic itso chaio
po ya quito lalaioga

Ruuanlos yns an Jamar cas y
soras lucanas. pari na corpac.
ala guerra ybatalla Sepric:
sa lollilian

The conquering Inca goes into battle on a litter.

A GRAND WAY TO GO

No one who saw the arrival of the Inca—as the ruler of the Incan people was called —ferried in his lavishly contrived litter, was likely to forget it. "Atahualpa came in a very fine litter with the ends of its timbers covered in silver," wrote one astonished Spaniard. This early status symbol would also boast the rare Spondylus shells found in Ecuador, a favorite province of Atahualpa's father, Huayna Capac. Incan litters served a military as well as a political purpose. As one chronicle recounted in 1587: "The Inca fights from his litter, and uses his sling to hurl stones of precious gold at the enemy...." Lesser nobles, too, had the right to use litters. They were mortified when a Spanish decree of 1556 forbade them this exercise of power.

hillside over the city, conscripting twenty thousand laborers to quarry, cut, and haul the stones for the project. Along the face of the hill, three zigzagging walls rose up, one behind the other, to a height of sixty feet. Behind the walls Pachacuti erected three towers, linked by tunnels. The Inca provided the fortress with reservoirs and food storehouses so that the entire population of Cuzco could take refuge there in the event of a siege.

Sacsahuamán, the walls of which still stand, reveals the Incas' genius for working stone. Their temples, terraces, and roads have withstood earthquakes and centuries of use. In building these monumental structures, Incan masons first cut each stone into the approximate shape required. The masons then ground away at the stone as if it were a huge jewel, probably using wet sand as an abrasive. They repeatedly tested the stone's shape by levering it in and out of position and sanded it down until they achieved a fit so accurate that even a knife blade could not slip between the stones. Some of the stones that the Incas fitted in this meticulous way were of tremendous size: in the walls of Pachacuti's fortress there is a stone that weighs an estimated 128 tons.

As Pachacuti was building Sacsahuamán, he was also erecting a great palace for himself, with a silver-clad gateway and an immense audience hall about two hundred yards long. Each succeeding emperor built his own stone palace and filled it with treasures of silver and gold that glorified him both in life and in death. On his death each emperor was mummified and laid to rest in his palace, where women were employed to do nothing else but swish flies away from the wizened corpse. Every day attendants sat the mummy on a throne, raised the throne onto a litter, and paraded the dead Inca through the main plaza of Cuzco.

Just south of this plaza stood the greatest treasure-house of the capital, the Temple of the Sun. A square structure of stone, the temple was about two hundred feet long and sheathed in hundreds of gold plates. An eight-inch-high frieze of gold ran around the temple at roof level. Within the temple six chapels held a fabulous lode of gold, including the most precious and most sacred object in the em-

TEXT CONTINUED ON PAGE 86

The city of Machu Picchu is so high among the remote, mist-shrouded peaks of the Andes that the Spaniards never found nor even learned of it.

THE TOP OF THE WORLD

Machu Picchu, a city hewn of solid granite, seems to boast the standard features of any of the well-designed, small towns set throughout the Inca Empire. A road leads directly to it from Cuzco, the capital, in the south. Its one-hundred-acre site is filled with plazas, bathhouses, fountains, gardens, and points of government and religious administration. At the center appears to be a temple to the sun god, Inti. Sturdy walls combine with sheer mountain faces to make an impregnable fortress.

Yet, for all its disarmingly ordinary features, Machu Picchu is set nine thousand feet up on a secluded Andes saddleback—on an almost inaccessible spot, uninhabitable for all but a few months of the year. It might simply be one more small town but for the fact that such care and artistry have been lavished on its stonework to make it unique. It might be an outpost-fortress but for its apparent religious aura. It may be that some of the housing within the walls provided homes for the *acllacuna*, virgins of the sun chosen for their beauty. The Inca might have selected some of these young women as concubines for his or another noble's harem and reserved a few of them for occasional rituals of human sacrifice. But whether the city was built for the performance of such rituals—and for whose benefit they might have been performed—remains entirely unknown.

The severity of the peak Huayna Picchu, opposite, contrasts sharply with such ordinary domestic details as the thatched-roof dwelling pitched to withstand the area's frequent rainfall. Farmers used the terraces for the growing of maize, potatoes, and quinoa—a protein-rich mountain rice.

These monumental steps show the uncommon precision of Incan masonry. The smooth joints and true angles attest to the patience and expertise of artisans who had no iron or steel tools. To shape the granite they put a thin layer of wet sand between two stones and rubbed carefully.

Different styles of stonework converge at the doorway (right) of the so-called House of the Princess. The trapezoidal shape of the opening is typical of Incan architecture. Usually, large, irregular blocks such as those around the door would have been used for walls, terraces, or courtyard enclosures. The engineers preferred rectangular blocks for the main parts of a building. The odd projection just above the doorway, if not purely decorative, might be a peg for securing a wooden door, also attached to the two handles visible on either side.

This grotto beneath a tower at Machu Picchu—its eccentric steps leading nowhere—may have been a royal mausoleum. The Incas tended to the mummies of their princes and kings every day, carrying the preserved bodies in processions and offering them food, drink, and prayers.

The huge stone altar and post at Intihuatana, the "place to which the sun is tied," dominate the city; and devotion to the sun god himself,

ancestor of the Inca, was the duty of every citizen. Conquered tribes could keep their own gods if they acknowledged the sun's supremacy.

TEXT CONTINUED FROM PAGE 79

pire—the massive, jewel-encrusted, golden image of the sun itself.

Despite Cuzco's grandeur, the largest city in the Incan realm, ironically, was not one built by the Incas. The largest city was Chan Chan, a metropolis in northern Peru that had been the capital of the wealthy Chimú people, whose domain had extended for roughly six hundred miles along the northern Peruvian coast and had included the old Moche lands. Chan Chan was a colorful maze of brightly painted temples, residences, and plazas, covering about eleven square miles and bustling with a population of twenty-five to thirty thousand people. Many of these residents were craftsmen—weavers, potters, wood-carvers, painters, and goldsmiths.

The goldsmiths of Chan Chan produced sumptuous, delicate treasures for the city's aristocrats, who dressed in glittering splendor with necklaces, breastplates, and even fingertip covers of gold. A Chan Chan nobleman drank from a gold cup and plucked out his whiskers with tweezers of gold. When he was carried through the streets of the city on his litter, he leaned upon a backrest of gold.

When the Incas conquered the Chimú about 1470, they were dazzled by the treasures they found in Chan Chan. Packtrains of llamas carried off the city's gold and silver, and the goldsmiths themselves were marched off to the palaces of Cuzco to fashion precious objects for their new masters.

The Incas were able to enjoy in peace the golden fruits of their victory over the Chimú for more than fifty years, until a civil war threw the empire into a tumult. When the emperor Huayna Capac died, about 1525, there was a violent dispute between his sons Huáscar and Atahualpa over the succession. Huáscar was proclaimed Inca, but Atahualpa defeated Huáscar's forces. It was at this critical moment, with the Inca Empire riven by civil war and also decimated by a plague that may have resulted from contact with Europeans, that a small force of Spaniards landed on the northern coast of Peru, at Tumbes.

The Spanish had known of the existence of the Inca Empire and of its golden wealth for five years, since the time of the first exploratory voyages southward along the Ecuadorian and Peruvian coast-

This kneeling young woman weaves cloth upon a belt loom, one end of which would be fastened to a tree. Woven goods were practical, symbolic, and valuable, and each Incan household produced a required amount annually for the state.

lines. Now they returned, intent on conquest, under the command of a determined, experienced, and dauntless commander, Francisco Pizarro. He was past the age of fifty and could have been living a comfortable life in Panama, where he had settled in 1519; but an unrelenting ambition drove him into the unexplored lands of Peru, where he braved disease, hunger, and the threat of death with the toughness and iron will of a conqueror. He also had a rare talent for spotting a weakness and exploiting it to the hilt. As he marched south with 168 men, he learned of the Incan civil war from interpreters and planned to capitalize on the rift.

Atahualpa, at the head of a victorious army, had no reason to view the strange foreigners as a threat. Moreover, he was intrigued, especially by their horses, and allowed them to continue their advance. Pizarro arrived at the town of Cajamarca, near which Atahualpa was encamped, in November 1532.

On November 16, some five thousand Incas made their way in stately procession to the city. The emperor, carried on his gold-encrusted litter, planned on taking the foreigners captive, relying on sheer weight of numbers to do so. But as the Incas, in full ceremonial dress, with discs of gold and silver on their heads, moved into Cajamarca's central square, there was no one in sight. The Spaniards, many of them on horseback, were hidden within the buildings facing the square.

Once the square was packed with Incas, Pizarro's chaplain, the Dominican friar Vincente de Valverde, walked out to confront Atahualpa. Through an interpreter Valverde told the emperor that the pope had commissioned the Spanish to conquer and convert the inhabitants of America. Then he explained the tenets of Christianity, including the story of the crucifixion.

Atahualpa was not impressed by the power of the Christian God. "As for the Pope of whom you speak," Atahualpa replied to the priest, "he must be crazy to talk of giving away countries that do not belong to him. . . . Your god, as you say, was put to death by the very men he created. But mine," proclaimed Atahualpa, pointing to the sun, "still lives in the heavens."

An Incan accountant reads his quipu, a simple but ingenious device the Indians used to log information. The quipu—a series of strings coded by knots and colors—recorded censuses, harvest yields, inventories, even historical events. The accountants, being eloquent interpreters of the quipu, enjoyed great prestige in Incan society.

The sixteenth-century Flemish painter Théodore de Bry imaginatively but inaccurately portrayed the amassing of Atahualpa's ransom, above. He had never seen an Indian but does capture the European fascination with the booty, which totaled over six tons of solid gold and thirteen tons of silver—enough to enrich Spain and cause inflation in western Europe.

De Bry invents suitable Incan revenge with molten gold.

A KING'S RANSOM

Mounting an ambush at a supposedly diplomatic encounter, Francisco Pizarro, the Spanish conquistador, exploited his advantages—surprise, superior weaponry, and the cavalry horse—to massacre thousands of stunned Incas in Atahualpa's entourage and take the Inca himself prisoner. Atahualpa's courage shone in the reply he was said to have made to the Spaniard's invitation to dinner: "Do not console me, Captain. I know that the purpose of war is to conquer or be conquered." Nonetheless, he was soon bargaining for his release by offering to collect enough gold to fill a room twenty-two feet long by seventeen wide. He promised silver enough to fill another room twice. Atahualpa's loyal subjects brought fabulously worked vessels and other precious objects to pay the ransom, but the Spaniards did not keep the bargain. Pizarro distributed portions of the ransom among his soldiers and then, fearing that an Incan army might come to rescue their lord, he executed Atahualpa in the central square of Cajamarca before his helpless people. Embittered, the Incas hid uncounted rich treasure, perhaps for all time.

Atahualpa asked to see the prayer book Valverde was holding. The Inca examined it closely, intrigued by the lines of words and the pictures; then he threw it to the ground in disgust. Appalled, Valverde called out to Pizarro to attack.

Suddenly a cannon fired. Trumpets blared. With war cries, horsemen exploded from the doorways. The Incas, assailed by the noise and towering horses, panicked. Atahualpa's guards, leaping to his defense, were cut down as Spaniards seized the emperor. Other horsemen, wheeling among the packed and struggling Incas, killed them "like a slaughterer fells cattle," as Atahualpa's nephew later described the scene. In two hours the meager number of Spaniards killed several thousand Incas and left their army shattered, demoralized, and leaderless.

After his initial shock at this sudden reversal, Atahualpa took note of what the Spanish were after. The victors pillaged his abandoned camp, bringing back 800 pounds of gold and 3,500 pounds of silver—effigies, dishes, pitchers, and cups. The emperor, thinking that he might buy both his own freedom and the Spaniards' departure, then made Pizarro a staggering offer. He said that he would ransom himself by filling his prison cell, some twenty-two feet long by seventeen feet across, with golden objects to a height about eight feet from the floor. In addition he pledged twice that amount in silver. Pizarro, amazed, immediately accepted the deal, and Atahualpa became a cooperative hostage, issuing orders from his prison for the collection of gold throughout the empire and also guaranteeing the safety of the Spaniards.

Over the next few weeks, the treasure began to trickle in, somewhat too slowly for the impatient Spaniards. The emperor suggested they go to Cuzco themselves and speed things up by seizing gold from the Temple of the Sun. They did so, prying from the walls seven hundred of the golden plates, which weighed four and a half pounds each. Atahualpa's generals, with perhaps sixty-five thousand men under arms, obeyed their lord and did nothing to prevent the desecration of this, their most sacred temple.

In June the melting began. Incan smiths working with nine

Devious and persistent, Francisco Pizarro conquered a world empire with a small band of weary, frightened, and untrustworthy adventurers. In this oil portrait his elegant dress confers an aura of aristocracy upon this self-made man.

furnaces melted down thousands of objects a day, until they had reduced a treasure trove of priceless artifacts to about twenty tons of gold and silver bars. In the same month two more trains of llamas arrived from Cuzco bearing another twelve tons of treasure. By then Atahualpa's presence seemed to many Spaniards an increasing danger. Rumors spread that a great army was on its way to rescue him, and a number of the invaders argued that it would be safer to kill Atahualpa and head on to Cuzco.

On Saturday, July 26, 1533, Atahualpa was led out into the square in Cajamarca to be burned alive. He was tied to a stake while Valverde, the same priest who had confronted Atahualpa on this very spot eight months before, once again attempted to convert the Inca. This time Valverde's words carried a greater urgency, for he told Atahualpa that if he converted to Christianity he would not be burned, but strangled. Faced with this grim dilemma, Atahualpa chose the less painful death. He was baptized Juan de Atahualpa and then strangled.

Thereafter, the leaderless empire fell easy prey to the Spaniards, who looted and pillaged their way southward. In Cuzco they seized another six thousand pounds of gold and fifty thousand pounds of silver, though they never discovered the great golden image of the sun, which the Incas had managed to spirit out of its temple. The sacred image has never been found.

The Spanish conquest brought little good and a great deal of harm. A few hundred Spaniards became millionaires, but the huge inpouring of gold created ruinous inflation in Europe. In Peru the conquest had a cataclysmic effect. In the fifty years following Atahualpa's death, the whole fabric of the state collapsed. Irrigation works failed, roads crumbled, storehouses stood empty, disease spread, and people starved. The population dropped from an estimated six million to about two million.

Vestiges of the empire have survived: great stone temples, bastions, palaces, and highways. Even in ruins these monuments retain the majesty and dignity of the splendid empire of the Incas—rich in gold, proud, and tragic.

OVERLOOKED TREASURE

*Conquering Incas seized much Chimú gold, like this dou-
ble-spouted waterpot studded with heads. The mysteriously
horned beasts at the sides are stylized felines.*

When the warlords of Cuzco successfully overran Chan Chan, capital of the mighty Chimú civilization, they brought home a fabulous treasure—gold and silver ornaments more ingenious and graceful than any the Incas had ever owned. More importantly, they also returned with many prisoners, probably including the state-supported artisans who had perfected the Chimú techniques and characteristic style. Within decades, ironically, all the beautiful metalwork they did for their Incan masters—and the Incan work as well—would be lost to the Spaniards.

When the Chimú kingdom fell, some portion of its hoard lay hidden in the lavishly furnished tombs of the nobility and thus escaped the conquerors. Here and on the following pages, the finest of those pieces glitter. The metalsmiths who fashioned these masks, gloves, and plaques used a sheet-metal technique, cutting and shaping flat sheets to produce their exquisite designs. Their only tools were stones of varying sizes. For complicated forms the craftsmen might use rivets, staples, or clamps to make attachments. Frequently they soldered. Their artistry no doubt helped devise the downfall of their kingdom: the Incas sought Chimú gold as the Spaniards later sought the Incas' gold. And from the tombs of the vanquished kingdom would come the only testimony to imperial Incan tastes.

This embossed funerary mask covered the face of a noble. An artisan pressed out facial features from the reverse side; then he added the repoussé discs and the resin pupils, from which fourteen emeralds hang in simulation of tears. Attendants sewed the mask to the top of a basketwork coffin.

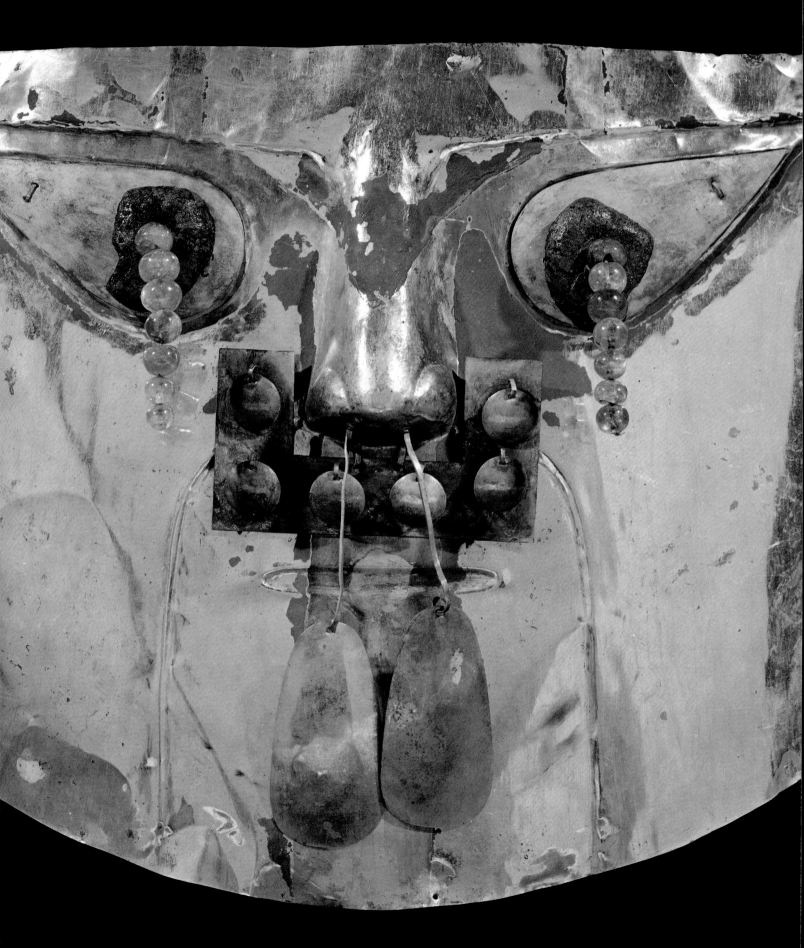

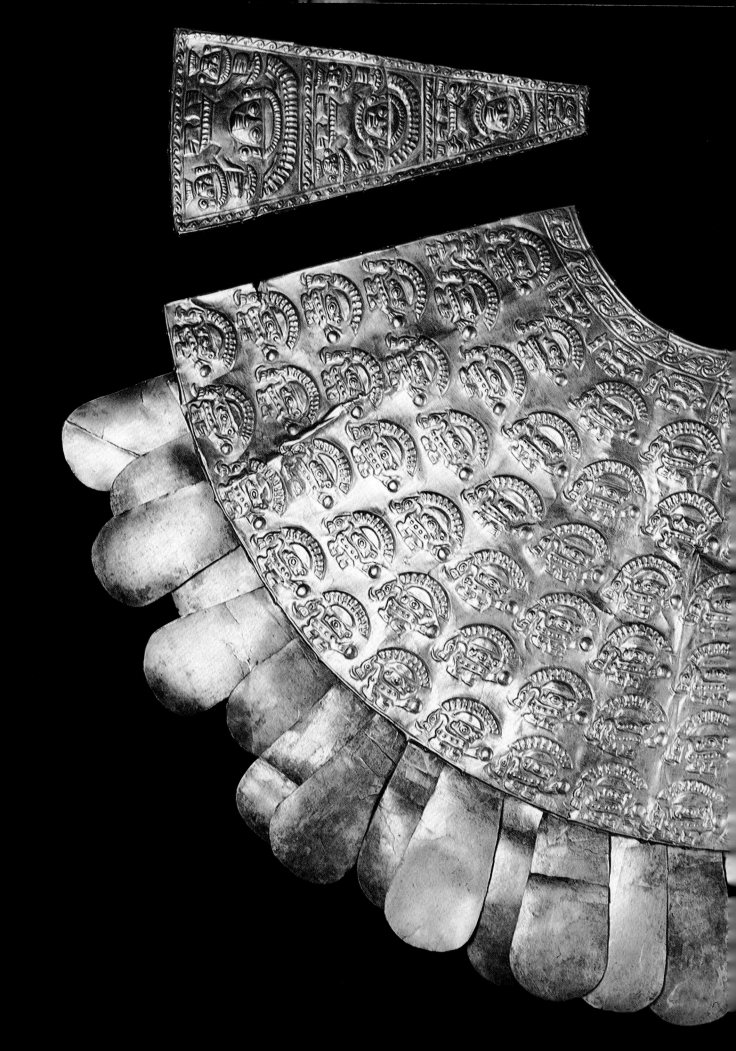

In this spectacular fringed collar with separate epaulets, a king—possibly the figure embossed into the gold jewelry—presided over great ritual occasions in Chimú ceremonial centers. Completing his ensemble with golden earplugs, nosepiece, necklace, and crown, the decorated ruler would radiate a dazzling presence in the sun.

Slanted eyes, earplugs, and regal headdress identify the central figure on the gold crown at left as a Chimú deity or ruler. From his hands hang severed heads, their traditional trophies of war. Few ever saw such gleaming surfaces because artisans frequently painted over gold objects and hid them in tombs.

A greenish band of copper edges the separate structural elements of the grand symbol of earthly power opposite—a cylindrical crown about two feet tall and a foot in diameter. Colorfully dyed cotton wool covered the band in order to highlight the scores of fluttering gold discs that are attached by gold staples.

Thousands of golden plaques, individually fastened onto striped fabric, make this tunic shimmer. The Chimú leader who owned the tunic may not have worn it in life—the gold appliqué being too heavy for comfort—but reserved it as a glittering burial robe. The Chimú probably forbade women to wear a costume this elaborate and expensive.

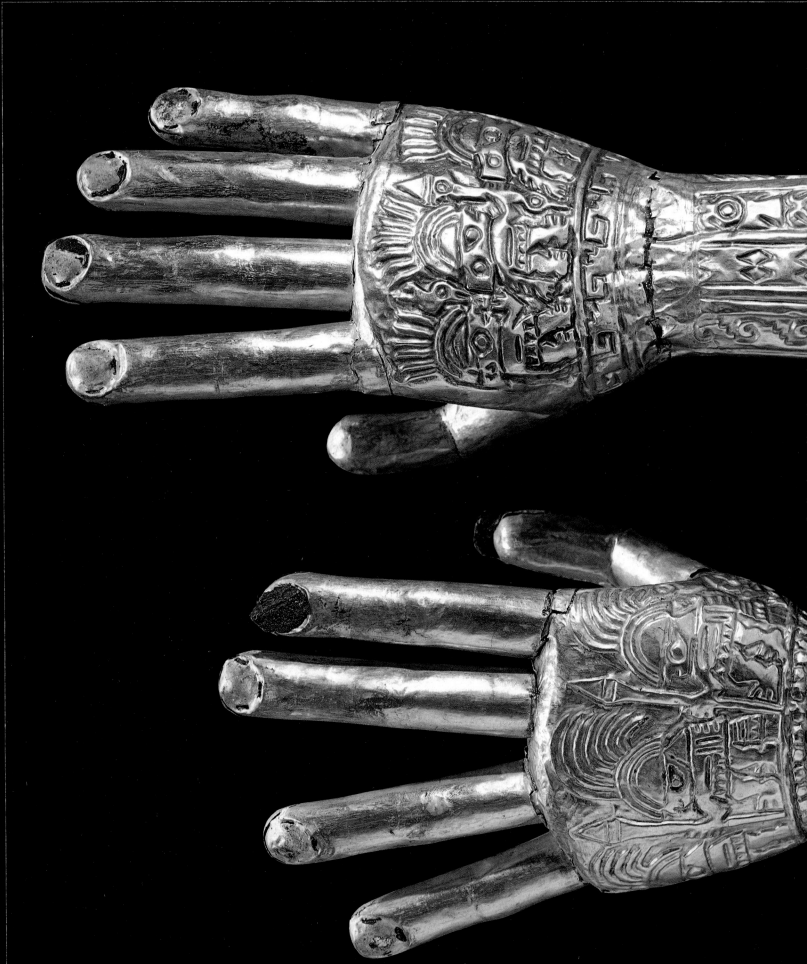

Chimú kings may have gone to their graves
with golden gloves slipped over their hands. This
exquisite pair, from the twelfth or thirteenth
century, was originally tipped with silver fingernails. On the backs of the hands, warriors sport
headdresses, and the forearms bear longitudinal
bands embossed with geometric patterns.

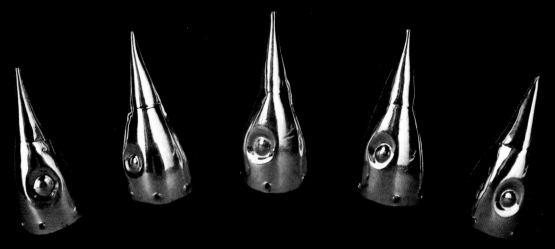

These golden birds' heads may have covered the fingertips of a Chimú king, the long beaks cast as nails. The five fingernail covers were probably part of the king's ceremonial regalia.

Chimú noblemen wore enormous earplugs as insignia of high rank. This pair of gold plugs has discs five and one-half inches in diameter, which are covered with hunting scenes. The finely incised tubes fit into the nobleman's earlobes, the flesh pierced and stretched to exaggerated proportions to accommodate the high-status ornaments.

DOUBLE-BOTTOMED CUP

CUP WITH WARRIOR

Chimú kings enjoyed a frothy beer made from maize and may have drunk their brew out of fine gold vessels such as these, from a royal tomb in Peru. The cups are encrusted with turquoise, and line patterns and warrior portraits are raised into the metal. The cup above has a double bottom, and the hollow chamber held a few small stones. Rattling it, the king who owned the cup commanded his servant to bring more beer.

Ancient Peruvian knives—sometimes called tumis—had narrow, elaborately topped handles and semicircular blades, such as the six on these pages, all from the twelfth to the fifteenth centuries. Fashioned of gold and most often set with turquoise, these knives, too fine for everyday use, were conspicuous badges of rank and power. The noblemen—warriors or kings who owned the knives—carried them as scepters or hung them from belts and necklaces. The simple blades are crowned with animals, men, and deities—each figure richly worked from gold and then decorated with more of the precious metal.

OVERLEAF: *In a detail of another knife, a fierce ruler holds discs of gold and turquoise in his hands. The man's filigreed headdress, large ear-plugs, and powerful countenance mark him as a king, if not a god.*

IV

THE GOLDEN WARRIORS

LORDS OF COLOMBIA

I n the Calima area of central Colombia, on the broad upper reaches of the Cauca River valley, there lived for many centuries a tribe of Indian maize farmers. At some time between the first and seventh centuries A.D., a great chief of this people died. As was the custom his mourners began to dig a vertical burial shaft a few feet across, loosening the dirt with sticks and carting it away in baskets. When the shaft was about fifteen feet deep, they hollowed out a little room some eight feet long and three feet across.

Meanwhile other mourners arranged for the manufacture of those objects that would assure their leader of acceptance in the afterlife—hunting gear, food, and other paraphernalia that proclaimed his high status. Goldsmiths hammered out a helmet, rings, and a decoration for the ruler's chest. A carpenter carved a stool like the one the chief had used during his life. One of his sons made a stick for hurling darts. The leader's wife and daughters made pots and pre-pared food for him, even giving him a ladle for his maize beer. The pots were symbolically killed by having holes drilled in them.

The painted warrior at left stalked the gold-laden Cauca River valley in Colombia, perhaps in A.D. 1000. The ceramic figure, with its slit eyes, seems sated and calm.

The mourners carefully laid the body out on the floor of the little vault and arrayed the dead chief with his golden helmet, rings, and pectoral. Around him they placed the stool, throwing-stick, food, and pots. The mourners crawled out of the vault, closed the entrance with stakes, and filled the shaft with earth. The flesh and food rotted away, but the chief's golden symbols of wealth remained little changed until their rediscovery.

The grave of this anonymous chief was like thousands of others in the dozens of tribal areas that made up Colombia between about 1000 B.C. and the sixteenth century A.D. Here there were no great empires, no massive stone temples, none of the great political and social units that rose and fell farther to the south. Colombia is not a land that encourages empire building. The size of France, Spain, and Portugal together, it is an extraordinarily varied mosaic of landscapes. In Colombia the Andes divides into three huge ranges that fan out northward, forming high, cold plateaus alternating with warm, welcoming valleys. Precipitous slopes drop down to two major rivers, the Cauca and the Magdalena. To the east lie hot grassy plains, to the southeast the Amazon rain forest. On the Caribbean coast, flat sands and rolling savannas give way to a lump of mountains—the Sierra Nevada de Santa Marta. On the Pacific coast, dense, tangled forests and swamps run south to Ecuador.

The region around the Calima River was one of several in Colombia where the inhabitants wrought objects of gold. Two other regions famous for their gold are the Tolima—the name of a section of modern Colombia on the Magdalena River—and the Quimbaya, named after an Indian tribe. Each of these regions was the homeland for a number of tribes whose histories remain, for the most part, unknown. Thus the precious objects buried with the chiefs of these tribes are a tantalizing legacy, for these treasures are certainly the work of imaginative and vigorous peoples.

An aura of mystery haunts the gold treasures of the Colombians. Some figures are part man, part beast. A human head may have immense, frightening inhuman jaws. A man might be flat, and his arms reduced to bonelike sticks—yet the mouth opens to speak, as if

Two Indians search for gold at the bank of a jungle river. The miner at left holds above his head a batea—a wooden tray used to wash the gold he collects—while his partner, hoping to find underground veins of the metal, breaks earth with a stick.

a skeleton refused to yield to death. Such were the gold objects the Colombians offered to their gods, and that chiefs, nobles, and priests took with them to their graves. The mysteriousness of the golden treasures is heightened further because little is known of the peoples who made them, or of the religions and myths that inspired these otherworldly splendors.

Before about 700 B.C. the Colombian Indians lived mostly along the coast, subsisting on fish and manioc, a tuber the Indians crushed and cooked to make flat cakes rich in protein. Dry manioc cakes could be stored for months without spoilage and for this reason were an important item of trade.

A change in the climate about 700 B.C. made possible the cultivation of an even better food—maize. Increasing rainfall made Colombia more hospitable to maize, which was probably introduced to the region by Indians from ancient Mexico who migrated to South America by sea on rafts. The cultivation of maize brought profound changes to the Colombians' way of life. Because maize could be grown on the slopes of mountains, the Colombians were able to break away from their dependence on the seacoast and to spread out into the interior. Population began to increase, and the previously homogenous culture of the Colombians blossomed into separate civilizations.

The Colombians who settled the interior found that their lands were rich in gold. The rivers that flowed down from the Andes into the Cauca and Magdalena glittered with gold-bearing rocks. About the beginning of the first century A.D., the Colombians learned how to extract and work this gold. They panned the silt of the river bottoms to retrieve the gold when the rivers were low, and they strung nets across the river to catch the gold when the rivers were at full flood. The dry land also yielded up its gold—the Colombians set fires to burn away the trees and brush and poked through the ashes until their eyes caught sight of the precious glitter. When the Colombians discovered that gold was often found near quartz, they dug shaft mines sixty to eighty feet deep, following the veins of quartz until they struck gold. One miner at a time crawled down into a shaft, filled a basket with ore, and then crawled out backward—the shafts were too narrow for a miner to turn around in.

The Indians gathered the gold-bearing rocks and ground them up on stones to break away the rock. They heated the small nuggets of gold in clay crucibles over a bed of charcoal. The goldworkers blew air onto the coals through narrow tubes to increase the temperature of the fire until the gold melted, at about 1,945 degrees. This temperature was difficult to attain, and the Colombian goldsmiths found that by adding copper to the gold they could lower the melting point of the metal by about one-fourth. A copper-and-gold alloy, sometimes with traces of silver, known as *tumbaga*, was the material most often used by Colombian goldsmiths.

The simplest method used by the Colombians to make gold objects was hammering. They placed a piece of gold on a stone anvil and hammered it until they made a broad, thin sheet, in which they could press designs. As they hammered the piece, they frequently annealed it—heated it to a red glow, then cooled it quickly with water—to prevent the gold from becoming brittle.

The Colombians possessed a remarkably sophisticated knowledge of metallurgy. For example, they were able to join two pieces of hammered gold by using a solution of copper dissolved in vinegar. First they bonded the two pieces with animal glue. Then they added a drop of the copper solution to the seam. When they heated the piece—a tricky operation that required a temperature just below the point at which the whole piece would be ruined—the copper fused with the gold. Colombian goldsmiths were also able to make a tumbaga object take on the appearance of pure gold by rubbing it with an acidic mineral or plant juice—the exact ingredient is unknown—and heating it. The acid in the mineral or juice removed the copper from the surface of the piece but left the gold intact.

Colombian goldsmiths fashioned many pieces with exquisitely delicate details using the so-called lost-wax process. The goldsmith made a model of the desired ornament in beeswax, coated it with clay, and heated it so that the wax melted and flowed out of the clay—leaving an impression on the inside of the clay. The smith

Feather-skirted natives, their long hair tucked into caps, melt gold, copper, and a bit of silver into the alloy tumbaga *to cast golden images. In this fanciful sixteenth-century European illustration, one smith stirs the molten metal, while his assistants gather more raw elements, tend the fire, and remove finished sculptures from their molds.*

poured molten gold into the clay mold, allowed it to cool, then broke the clay mold to reveal the finished object of solid gold.

A variation of the lost-wax technique allowed a goldsmith to make hollow objects. He first made a core of clay in the rough shape of the object he wanted, coated it with beeswax, and shaped the wax with all the fine details. The smith inserted several small pegs into this model and coated the model with another layer of clay. When the goldsmith melted out the wax, the pegs held the inner core in its place. After pouring in the molten gold, the smith broke the outer mold, removed the pegs, and carefully scraped out the inner clay core from the hollow gold piece. As a final touch he sealed up the peg holes with bits of gold.

Quimbaya goldsmiths used the lost-wax method to fashion superb golden bottles to hold the lime they took when chewing coca leaves. These luxury objects—some of them were about a foot high—were sometimes cast in the shape of naked men and women whose eyes are closed and whose faces bear the dreamy, calm expression of a drug-induced trance.

The goldsmiths of the Calima region also wrought elegant drug implements. They excelled at making miniature, jewellike statuettes to decorate the tops of lime-dippers—the pins used to transfer lime from the pot to the coca chewer's mouth. The delicate figurines represent animals, chiefs, and priests. Some of the human figures even have tiny moving jewelry on their noses. The Calima goldsmiths were also masters of hammering gold. They fashioned imposing nose ornaments, so wide that they would have covered the whole lower portion of the wearer's face, with a long fringe of gold pieces dangling from the bottom.

The goldworking techniques and the customs of the Colombian tribes were described in an account written by the Spanish adventurer Pedro de Cieza de León, who first came to the New World as a teenager in 1532. Later he accompanied the expeditions of several conquistadors to Colombia. He survived hunger, a perilous passage over a mountain range where men and horses often tumbled to their deaths, the attacks of Indians, and the equally violent disputes

TEXT CONTINUED ON PAGE 120

STONE GODS AND TOMBSTONES

B y 500 B.C. primitive Indians had established a string of thriving farming villages in the forested hills near the headwaters of the Magdalena River—an area known today as San Agustín. After the first century A.D. there were sculptors among the farmers, too, and the agricultural settlements—which sprawled over nearly two hundred square miles—supported a ceremonial center that was punctuated by stone shafts and great statues of men, animals, and monsters. The San Agustín sculptors made over 320 statues, some of them marking enormous burial mounds called barrows, others guarding underground tombs.

The statues, some ten feet tall, dot the undulating greens at San Agustín. Though they lacked metal tools, the sculptors worked the stone by mauling and pecking it with smaller rocks and used abrasive sands to polish each sculpture.

The nature of the religious activities at San Agustín remains a mystery, but the fanged half-man, half-jaguar—an image that shamans of the society may have conjured from the feared jungle cat and certainly one that inspired the sculptors— was probably the focus of many of the ceremonies. Whatever role the strange statuary played at San Agustín, the stone "jaguar-men" and double-headed warriors manifested awesome power: when a Franciscan friar came upon the sculptures in the eighteenth century, he declared that only the devil himself could have made such horrifying creatures.

A helmeted "jaguar-man" bares his fangs in a forest clearing at San Agustín. The ancient stone monster sticks out his tongue, which ends in the head of a replica of the "jaguar-man" himself.

Cavernous tombs lie beneath the stone shafts at a San Agustín barrow, a green graveyard over eighty feet in diameter. The triangular

face opposite—part man, part jaguar in relief—is over seven feet tall, a likely focus of worship amid the soft, grassy burial mounds.

The serene reclining figure above is a relief sculpture on the lid of a sarcophagus, in an elaborate burial possibly reserved for chiefs and shamans of San Agustín. The workmanship of the subterranean chamber is as exacting as that of the sculpted coffin: the artist even polished the tomb walls in order to remove tool marks from the stone.

A stone warrior crosses his chest with a heavy club while balancing a squat version of himself on his head: together they protect the sacred grounds at San Agustín. A "jaguar-man" stands behind the ten-foot-high double guardian statue.

TEXT CONTINUED FROM PAGE 113

among the conquerors themselves. Despite the rigors of a wilderness campaign, Cieza de León wrote down meticulously detailed descriptions of the Indians' way of life.

Cieza de León found the Quimbaya tribe to be "well disposed, and of good countenance," though the nearly naked women were a little too "amorous" for his Christian sense of morality. He noted that the Quimbaya were fond of war, staging mock battles for recreation. When two villages met for a feast, the men drank their fill of maize beer and formed two opposing lines, with their women behind them. With cries of "we play!" the men raced back and forth hurling darts at each other. The barbs were real—when the players left the field at the end of the game, each side had to carry off several dead and wounded men.

But what impressed Cieza de León most of all was the wealth of the Colombians. "All the rivers are very full of gold," he wrote, also saying that "of all the things that were to be seen, the most notable were their jewels of gold and the great vases out of which they drink their wine." Even the warriors went into battle clad in gold. "When they go to war they wear crowns with beautiful plumes, with plates on their breasts, armlets, and many other ornaments. . . . I remember we saw armed Indians covered with gold from head to foot."

The warriors who arrayed themselves so opulently were nonetheless fierce and skilled in using a variety of lethal weapons, including lances, bows and arrows, slingshots, and blowguns. Blowguns were narrow tubes of cane from which a warrior could fire a dart with just a slight puff and accurately hit a small bird thirty or forty yards away. Blowguns were most useful in dense forests. On clear ground, where a man could freely swing his arm, warriors often used throwing-sticks to hurl their darts. A throwing-stick was a three-foot-long shaft of wood with a sharp piece of bone at one end. The warrior impaled a dart on the bone, and then he whipped the stick with an over-the-shoulder motion to fling the dart at his target.

The Indians used blowguns and throwing-sticks mostly for hunting small animals. For warfare they used the bow and arrow, smearing the tips with a deadly poison. Cieza de León found that one

While a metalsmith hammers out pure gold—preparatory to working the sheet into a spectacular piece of flat jewelry—his two assistants fan the brazier with their breath to liquify more precious nuggets. A young boy, who may be an apprentice, watches the three artists at work.

Colombian tribe prepared the poison for their arrows according to an elaborate formula that sounds like the recipe for an infernal witch's brew. First they chopped up the roots of a certain tree that grew by the ocean. They burned the pieces and mashed the remains into a paste. To this they added poisonous ants, spiders, worms, pieces of bats' wings, the heads and tails of poisonous fish and snakes, and finally a few poisonous apples. The last step in the preparation of the poison was perilous. "They prepare a great fire in a place far from their homes, and take some slave girl whom they do not value, and make her watch the pots, and attend to the brewing of the poison; but the smell kills the person who thus makes the juice."

Tribes often went to war to capture victims for religious sacrifices. Cieza de León described how prisoners were hauled onto platforms where their hearts were cut out and offered to the gods—a rite remarkably similar to the sacrifices of the Aztecs of Mexico. This practice of offering human hearts to the gods may well have been imported to Colombia from Mexico by migrating Indians. Another Mexican custom that made its way to Colombia was the taking of heads by warriors as trophies. With perhaps a bit of exaggeration, Cieza de León reported that, "We found so many human heads at the doors of the chiefs' houses, that it seemed as if each one had been a butcher shop."

Cieza de León found much more that he disliked in the beliefs and habits of the Colombians. For example, he noted with both horror and moral condemnation that human sacrifice was practiced at the burial of a chief. "When one of the chiefs dies, the people mourn for many days, cut off the hair of his wives, kill those who were most beloved, and raise a tomb the size of a small hill, with an opening towards the rising sun. Within this great tomb they make a large vault, and here they put the body, wrapped in clothes, and the gold and arms the dead man had used when alive. Then they take the most beautiful of his wives and some servant lads, make them drunk from wine made with maize, and bury them alive in that vault, in order that the chief may go down to hell with companions."

Certainly the Colombian custom that most appalled Cieza de

León, and frightened the rest of the Spaniards as well, was cannibalism. Cieza de León's account makes no mention of any religious motivation for the consumption of human flesh, nor did he note any special ceremonies connected with it. Indeed, in a conversation with Cieza de León's commander, Juan de Vadillo, one Quimbaya chief displayed a remarkably blasé attitude toward eating another person. When Vadillo asked the chief why he had brought his wife along with him one evening, "the chief replied, in a gentle voice, looking him in the face, that he was going to eat her."

According to Cieza de León, the Quimbaya raided their neighbors and carried off women to bear children for the cooking pots. They were eaten, says the Spaniard, "with great relish." Cieza de León, who was the most inquiring and scrupulous of chroniclers, apparently never indulged in this Colombian custom himself, but he did hear of hungry Spanish soldiers who came upon a bubbling pot in an abandoned house, ate the stew, and found at the bottom the remains of a hand.

For all his abhorrence of cannibalism, Cieza de León believed that one victim, the Spanish commander Jorge de Robledo, had deserved his fate. Robledo had cruelly put Indians to death by shooting them with crossbows and setting dogs on them. When Robledo and another Spanish commander fought over who would rule the conquered Indians, Robledo lost and was hanged. His rival left Robledo's body to be eaten by the Indians. "God permitted," wrote Cieza de León with approval, "that he should... have for his tomb the bellies of the Indians."

The Quimbaya Indians were virtually exterminated by the Spanish, after resisting to the end. Another tribe chose to starve themselves to death rather than serve the Spanish. At the root of the disaster was gold. "Our only wish is to fill our pockets," wrote Cieza de León, in despair that the Spanish had forgotten their noble purpose: to convert the Indians to Catholicism. He saw the irony in the Spaniards' quest for gold. The harder they pressed the Indians for gold, the deeper the Indians concealed it—"vast are the treasures that are lost in these parts."

RITUALS
AND DREAMS

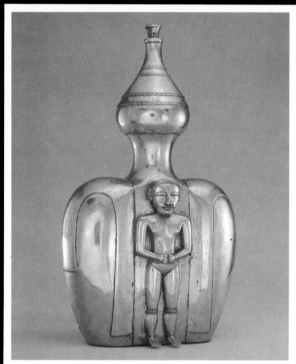

A woman, fists over her stomach, seems to guard this golden flask: the vessel is a container for lime powder, which Indians mixed with coca to induce euphoria.

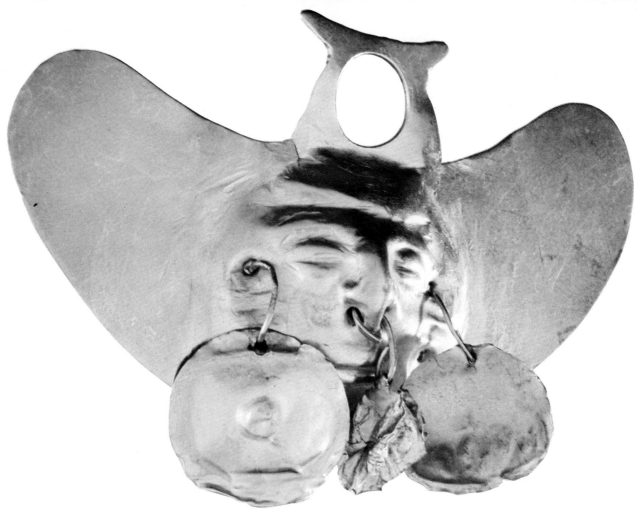

Ear and nose ornaments hang from a Calima chieftain, the centerpiece of a great golden earring.

So bloodthirsty that they would go to war simply for the sake of eating human flesh, the Indians of what is now western Colombia—the tribes of the Calima, Quimbaya, and Tolima regions—were insatiable in their love of gold as well. So, at least, said the Spaniards of the sixteenth century.

The area in which they lived was rich—legend had it that more gold than soil lay in the ground—and it was perhaps natural that these Indians should also become expert goldsmiths. The tribes had so much gold they even warred wearing crowns, breastplates, and armbands.

The smiths were privileged members of their society, and they employed many workers to gather gold and process it in their studios. The smiths worked both with pure gold and tumbaga, the malleable alloy of gold, copper, and sometimes traces of silver. Using both realistic and stylistic designs, the artists hammered out flat pieces of gold, which they cut into various shapes, then embossed, engraved, and filled with decorations. They embellished the gold with even more gold, adding dangling ornaments to flat jewelry and full-bodied sculptures.

Though revered chiefs and warriors chose to take many of these golden goods to their graves, the smiths also made things to delight the living. Since coca was one of the sublime pleasures of their world, the smiths made beautiful flasks and dippers for lime powder, which the leaders sprinkled on their lips when chewing the coca leaves.

A green-eyed Calima Indian chief seems to assert his wealth and power in this stylized portrait, which is also a nose ornament of extraordinary size: it is nine inches across. The artist first hammered out the oddly shaped pieces and then punched the gold, suspending glittering gold buttons in the hollows.

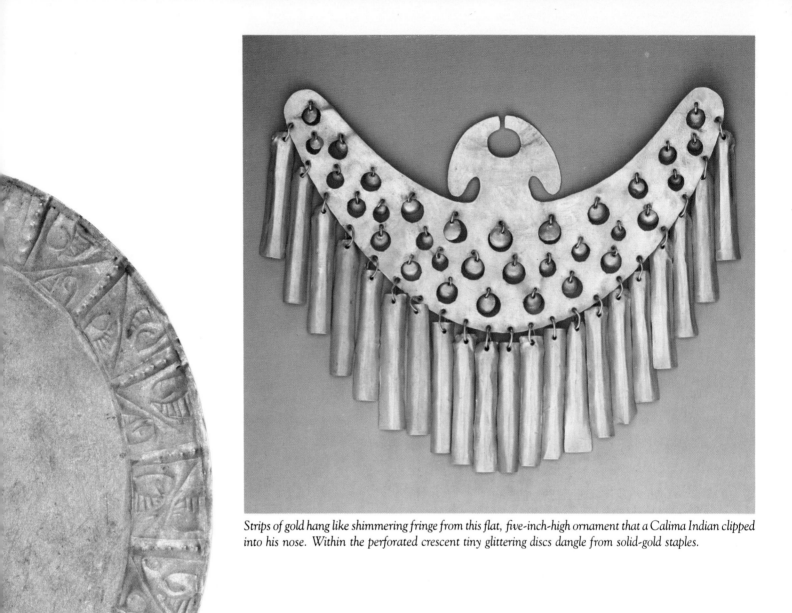

Strips of gold hang like shimmering fringe from this flat, five-inch-high ornament that a Calima Indian clipped into his nose. Within the perforated crescent tiny glittering discs dangle from solid-gold staples.

A man bedecked in gold jewelry placidly occupies the center of the seven-inch-wide breastplate at left, which a native smith hammered and chased from tumbaga. With the golden necklaces, earplugs, nose ornament, and diadem, the bust could be a royal portrait of the man who actually wore the breastplate—in life and in death.

A moonfaced chieftain blankly stares from his pectoral funerary mask. This portrait of a privileged Calima Indian, which fit over the chest, is made from a sheet of hammered gold.

Flashing sunlight, the diadem opposite gave its wearer a powerful luminescence. Two images within the foot-high headdress—the face surmounting the piece and the catlike figure raised in the center—are probably portraits of exalted warriors. A Calima smith made the headdress by cutting a large sheet of gold into a jagged design, embossing it, then stapling on the quivering, curling tinsel.

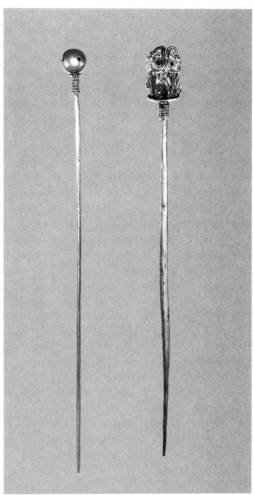

Noble Indians used long, slender sticks of gold—the shafts topped with intricate, intimate decorations, such as the bell at left above and the figure at right above—to add lime powder to coca leaves.

The three delicate sculptures at left crown lime-dippers, the precious paraphernalia of coca chewing. The beautifully plumed bird in the center is possibly a religious symbol; the figures flanking it may be portraits of royal warriors who are dressed, armed, and masked for ceremonial celebrations. The goldsmiths, who cast the dippers by the lost-wax process, worked the tiny original molds with wonderful details—none of which were lost on the molten metal.

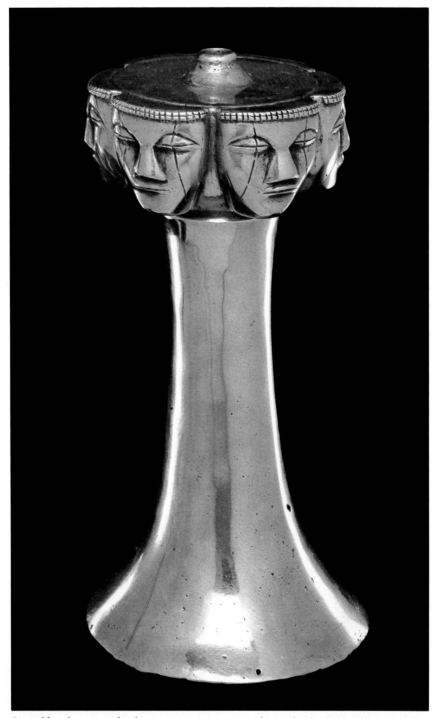

Six golden faces—each of serene expression—rim the neck of a flask. The vessel that would have been attached to the base contained lime, used to quicken the effect of coca.

A Quimbaya chieftain reposes in this golden mask, his earrings and nose ornament signaling his power and position. Mourners may have tied the mask, a tomb treasure, over the face of their ruler's corpse.

132

Wearing nothing but jewelry, these three squat sculptures are flasks that once held generous amounts of lime powder for their coca-chewing owners. Varying in height from five inches to over ten inches, the golden trio has in common tiny hands and feet, plaited coiffures, and otherworldly countenances. The figures mirror the Quimbaya, who took them to their graves: the seated man opposite has a lime flask of his own around his neck.

A Tolima man, his stepped limbs filled with cutout hatching, sports a crown and four round ornaments on his head. The splayed, insectlike figure is a ten-inch-wide pendant—a smith's masterpiece.

Zigzags through his flaring crown, the wiry leader opposite rests his hands across his stomach—at the center of what is a large pendant of abstract design. Four identical birds, two flanking the head and two at his feet, and a pair of crested creatures on the arms all seem to guard the small-mouthed man.

OVERLEAF: Even baring his teeth, the warrior above appears at peace: eyes closed, he may be feeling the effects of coca leaves touched with lime.

V

THE GILDED MAN

FOUND AND LOST AGAIN

What for a time promised to be the ultimate golden kingdom lay northeast of the Quimbaya and Tolima regions, in the very heart of ancient Colombia. This was the homeland of the Muisca, a civilization made up of numerous villages that extended across a high plateau of savannas, rich farmlands, and shimmering lagoons. To the Muisca many of these lagoons were sacred, and one of them—a round lake called Guatavita by the Spaniards—was very likely the site for an extraordinary ceremony that was held upon the appointment of a new ruler.

The young chieftain would make his way to the shore of this lake, where his people stripped him naked, applied a sticky resin to his body, and dusted him all over with powdered gold, which united with the resin to form a second glittering skin. Made brilliant by sunlight, and surrounded by minor chiefs, the golden man took his place on a raft, with heaps of gold and emeralds piled at his feet. The raft set off from shore to the sound of music from flutes and trumpets. When it reached the middle of the lake, a signal was given and all

This somber face is a mask from the kingdom of the Muisca, who lived near a sacred lagoon and may have been the people ruled by El Dorado, "the Gilded Man."

Members of a German-financed expedition to South America march outside the Spanish city of Seville before setting sail for Venezuela. From there a group led by Nikolaus Federmann forged into Colombia in 1537. His expedition was one of three to converge on the Muisca homeland within a year.

were silent as the chieftain lofted his treasures into the still water. The raft then made its way back, whereupon the music and shouting began again, and the people on shore received the golden man as their new lord and king.

Neither the origin of this ceremony, nor the date of its final occurrence, are at all certain. Various descriptions of it, however, seized the minds of hundreds of Spaniards and other Europeans in the sixteenth century. No European ever witnessed the ceremony. But the image of the shining ruler, whom the Spaniards called El Dorado—"the Gilded Man"—eventually lured adventurers into some of the harshest, most remote parts of Colombia in search of this king and his treasures.

What also fueled their quest was the quite visible wealth possessed by the Muisca and by other chiefdoms even farther north. The Muisca had occupied the central highlands for nearly a millennium before the first Spaniards arrived in Colombia, about 1500. Most of the Muisca settlements lay between eight and nine thousand feet above sea level—a cool, misty altitude that proved excellent for growing maize and potatoes, their two staples. As a result of the rich land, the countryside was dotted with neat farms, market centers, and villages of thatched huts that all together supported at least a million people.

Like the earlier Tolima and Calima cultures to the south, the Muisca—who have also been known as the Chibcha, after one of their gods—had no writing, no calendar, no stone buildings, and no network of roads. However, they did have a splendid capital near present-day Bogotá, from which a ruling lord, called the Zipa, governed the southern portion of Muisca territory. This ancient capital was a city of wooden palaces for the nobility, each palace constructed of walls of woven cane and high conical thatched roofs topped by long masts that were dyed red. To the northeast, near the modern town of Tunja, stood a second capital that was the home of the Zacque, another paramount lord. Most of the Muisca villages were organized into two loose federations under these rulers.

The demand for gold among the Muisca matched that in any of

the other great Andean cultures. Yet no natural sources of the metal existed within the Muisca homeland. Instead, raw gold had to be imported from tribes to the north, in the valley of the Magdalena River. In exchange for the gold, the Muisca offered cotton cloth, emeralds, and above all, salt, a precious commodity that was mined and turned into compact loaves.

Perhaps because gold was not readily available, Muisca smiths developed a distinctive style that would make the metal go as far as possible. For their jewelry they often combined gold with emeralds, stone beads, and parrot feathers. More characteristic were small, flat, slender figurines used as offerings to deities. These *tunjos,* as they are known, typically were made from gold or a copper-gold alloy, and each consisted of a plaque on which the artisan added details in wirelike threads cast from wax. Though simpler and plainer than other forms of goldwork, the tunjos portray the Muisca people: warriors, mothers with children, coca chewers, priests, and chieftains. And there exists one magnificent tunjo that shows nothing less than a chieftain and his attendants on a golden raft—a tableau that brilliantly evokes the ceremony on Lake Guatavita.

The Muisca were only one of three principal goldworking cultures that the Spanish encountered in the north. The vital trade route along the Magdalena River ended in the far north at the Tairona territory, homeland of the most formidable Colombian empire at the time of the conquest. As builders, the Tairona rivaled the Incas. Some three hundred years before the construction of Machu Picchu, they were creating considerably larger cities in the dense jungle foothills of the Sierra Nevada de Santa Marta.

One such site, abandoned to the jungle and discovered four hundred years later, contains a large central knoll, skillfully reinforced by thousands of stones, that gradually descends onto a wide ceremonial esplanade. Below this, flowing out in layers down the sides of the mountain, are man-made circular terraces created to provide flat surfaces for planting crops. The wood-and-thatch houses have disappeared, but other architectural marvels still in evidence include an intricate drainage system, reservoirs, bridges, a large rock

Gonzalo Jiménez de Quesada, arrayed in the regalia of a conquistador in this hand-colored engraving, led the largest expedition into Muisca territory. By 1538 he had subdued the Indians—an effort that cost him some five hundred men—and had looted their villages to amass a ton of fine gold.

tablet that might be a map of the city, and three hundred miles of intersecting stairways and roads.

Dozens of these jungle metropolises, some with a thousand or more dwellings, served as the capitals of ministates that supported a variety of skilled artisans. Stonecutters crafted finely shaped figurines of agate and quartz, and potters frequently displayed bird designs on their wares in a handsome black pigment made from crushed leaves. Tairona goldwork was bold and perfect, especially on small pendants that had human figures with gorgeous arching headdresses, fierce expressions, and golden ornaments dangling from their ears and noses. The people themselves surely wore such necklaces, crowns, and other jewels lavishly and with pride.

Just as stunning were the gold treasures from the kingdoms of the Sinú, a densely populated, enormously wealthy federation that controlled savannas near the Caribbean coast. Their principal city boasted large communal dwellings and a great temple, capable of holding a thousand people, that contained wooden idols covered with sheet gold. Outside the temple were the burial mounds of chieftains, topped by trees hung with golden bells.

Sinú goldsmiths were among the most skilled in South America. The gold they used, acquired in its raw state from farther inland, was extremely pure, containing some silver, but little copper. With it they cast figurines of land animals, birds, and aquatic creatures, as well as numerous vessels and elegant jewelry. Their most exquisite creations are semicircular ear ornaments with a lacy, netlike pattern that has the delicacy of filigree, though the ornaments were cast by the lost-wax method. Such finery came to be much in demand in other regions, and Sinú goldwork found its way not only inland and to the east in Tairona country, but also northward as far as Panama and Costa Rica. The gold was also buried with Sinú lords, in mounds as large as sixty yards across, which were stocked with nose and ear ornaments, bracelets, crowns, bells, and massive breastplates.

The discovery and looting of Sinú tombs by an expedition of Spaniards early in the 1530s helped trigger the first mad rush for gold in Colombia. Spanish ships had first explored the Colombian coast

Outside their camp, Spaniards brandishing swords battle Indians armed with clubs, slings, and bows. The German artist who painted this scene had never been to America and, unaware that the Indians were beardless, gave them all bearded faces.

in 1501, and in 1526 a city and port took shape at Santa Marta, close to the Tairona territory. From Santa Marta the Spaniards had begun invading Tairona villages in the 1520s, where they were fiercely resisted by warriors armed with axes and poisonous arrows. Nevertheless, the Spaniards managed to rob burial grounds: one raiding party in 1529 obtained some two hundred pounds of alloyed gold in a month. And when astonished explorers reached the more accessible Sinú provinces, they reported finding an equal amount of very fine gold in a single tomb. The incredible riches of the Sinú instantly created an atmosphere of greed and mistrust, so that after a few years of frantic activity the sepulchers and temples were practically exhausted. By then news of the riches in Incan Peru had reached the Caribbean, gold fever had swept back to Spain, and other explorations and raiding parties were rapidly organized to open up the vast interior of the land now called Castilla del Oro—"Golden Castille."

There were a dozen expeditions in as many years, most of them disastrous. Hundreds died of disease, starvation, and from poisonous arrows—the one weapon that truly terrified the Spaniards, for anyone seriously wounded died, raving and convulsing, within a few days. But the conquistadors and their sponsors were certain they would eventually find precious stones and metals to mine, kingdoms to loot, land to settle, and an alternative route to the Pacific. The expedition members, piratical riffraff of all nationalities, were also adventurers, but with a single goal. "They only come until they get gold," wrote a chronicler who accompanied several expeditions. "They subordinate honor, morality, and honesty to this end."

In April of 1536 the largest of these expeditions set out from Santa Marta commanded by Gonzalo Jiménez de Quesada, a thirty-six-year-old lawyer whose plan was to locate the source of the Magdalena River, thinking it might lead to Peru. Quesada may also have suspected that the mines supplying the Tairona with emeralds lay somewhere along this river. He divided his expeditionary force into two contingents and sent one upstream while he led a land party consisting of six hundred soldiers, eighty-five horses, priests, and several royal notaries to tally up the spoils.

The parties were to meet two hundred miles upriver, but almost at once several riverboats were wrecked, and Indians attacked both groups. Mosquitoes and rain tormented them, they were constantly hungry and ridden with fever, and death came not only from Indians, but from poisonous snakes and jaguars as well. The weary trekkers often buried their dead with unseemly haste. "Sometimes," wrote one historian of the march, "a hand clenched in its last agony...remained above the ground, seeming to wave farewell to those who went in search of that accursed gold."

Hacking through jungle and often up to their waists in swamps, the Spaniards took three months to cover seventy miles, and at least one hundred men had died by the time Quesada met up with the river fleet. The expedition continued upstream until the river became impassable. Along the way, however, Quesada discovered that local Indians possessed salt in the form of loaves, which he was told came from the lands of a powerful tribe to the east. So before turning back, the conquistador led a band of sixty men up the Opón river, a tributary flowing from the southeast.

One of his scouting parties, following the salt trail, stumbled upon villages at the northern perimeter of Muisca territory. The Indians there yielded both gold and emeralds to the Europeans. Quesada was overjoyed and assembled what was left of his forces—about 170 men and 70 horses—to conquer the entire Muisca empire.

He met little resistance at first. In the outlying villages the people were awed, especially by the mounted soldiers swathed in massive pads of cotton armor. The Indians kept their distance and also provided a steady supply of gold, which Quesada kept in chests at his lodging. When he at last approached the capital at Bogotá, the Zipa launched an attack with six hundred warriors, but the Spaniards easily won, their horses routing the Indian army like modern-day tanks. In April of 1537 the treasure hunters reached the Zipa's palace, only to find that the ruler had fled with most of his wealth.

Over the next year Quesada and his soldiers of fortune conquered most of the remaining towns, eventually returning to Bogotá with more than a ton of gold treasures, which they melted down and

In an imagined portrayal of El Dorado himself, an Indian ruler is covered with gold dust by attendants, one who smears him with resin and another who blows gold through a tube. The artist, Théodore de Bry, based his 1599 engraving on secondhand accounts of stories travelers gathered from the Indians.

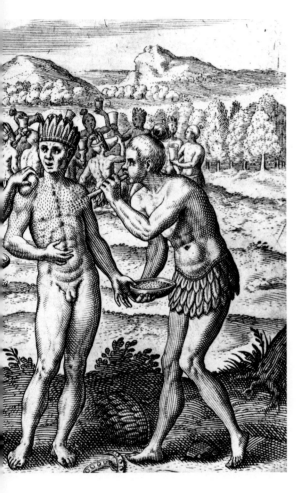

divided among themselves, with some two thousand emeralds. Possibly at this time, as he prepared to head back to Santa Marta, Quesada first heard about the Gilded Man and the ceremony at Lake Guatavita. But before he had a chance to confirm the story, he heard news that startled him even more: two other expeditions had marched into Muisca territory and were encamped nearby.

One of these expeditions, sponsored by German bankers, had approached from the northeast, coming down through Venezuela from the coastal city of Coro. The leader was a stocky, red-bearded, thirty-year-old German, Nikolaus Federmann, who had started out late in 1536 with three hundred men. During their westward passage through the high Cordillera, intense cold had killed most of the horses and Indian porters, and the survivors were badly exhausted when they reached a Muisca village a few miles from Bogotá.

By that point envoys of Quesada had encountered the third expedition, which entered Colombia from the south. This force was headed by Sebastián de Belalcázar, formerly a lieutenant of Pizarro's, and perhaps the first leader to have any notion of a golden man: much earlier his men had captured an Indian ruler they called *el indio dorado*. The information, however, did not inspire Belalcázar to rush. He had moved slowly toward Bogotá, taking along a huge caravan of livestock, soldiers, and five thousand Indians.

Thus, in February 1539, all three ambitious leaders were claiming authority over the Muisca. It was a tense situation, which Quesada defused by striking agreements whereby men from each expedition would be granted land to colonize. Afterward, the three explorers made their way to Cartagena and from there sailed to Spain to present their claims before King Charles I (who was, as Charles V, also Holy Roman Emperor).

Only Belalcázar was immediately successful: he received a governorship in southern Colombia, as well as a license to market cinnamon. Federmann became embroiled in law suits with his sponsors, which ended only when he died suddenly in 1542. And Quesada, who expected a hero's welcome, instead was accused by a hostile court of brutalizing the Indians and cheating the crown of its gold.

Whatever he and the others had heard about a golden man, they never acted on it. Yet within a few years of their return, the rumors of El Dorado spread quickly and galvanized other expeditions—even though the source of the rumors continued to be obscure. One historian traced the Gilded Man to Quito, for Spaniards there had heard from the Indians about a "great lord...continually covered in gold dust...who looks as resplendent as a gold object worked by the hand of a great artist." Other secondhand accounts mingled elements of Belalcázar's indio dorado with the ceremony at Lake Guatavita. With each telling the story grew more embellished, evolving from the report of a golden prince to the elaborate notion of a kingdom where virtually everything was made of gold. And it was to the legend, not the facts, that the historians, explorers, and officials of Spain and other countries responded.

In the 1540s expeditions went into unexplored regions of Peru, Colombia, and Ecuador. Pizarro's brother, Gonzalo, led a disastrous effort from Quito to find the fabled kingdom. A brother of Quesada's also organized a force, and in 1569 Quesada himself set out on a second, grander conquest. He found nothing: nor did other adventurers—among them the great English navigator Sir Walter Raleigh—who pursued El Dorado all the way from Panama to Guyana over the next half century.

Even then the dream refused to die. Unable to find a golden kingdom, treasure seekers returned again and again to the legend's foremost point of origin, Lake Guatavita. In the 1580s a Spanish merchant made the most ambitious attempt to drain the lake, employing eight thousand Indians to cut an immense notch in the crater walls. The water level sank by sixty feet, his men found some gold discs and emeralds and then the walls collapsed, killing many of the workers. Other attempts followed, yet aside from a handful of gold jewelry, all they turned up was the thick mud of the lake bottom. But the troves of gold unearthed by grave robbers in the tombs of the Muisca, Tairona, and Sinú keep alive the legend of El Dorado: "the celebrated name," aptly concluded one chronicler, "which has cost so many lives and fortunes."

THE GOLD OF
EL DORADO

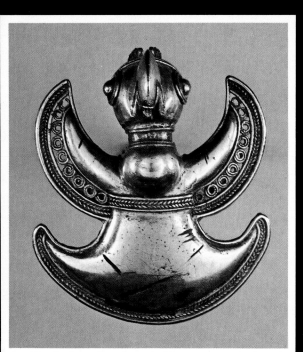

A golden bird-pendant from the Tairona region displays the mastery at casting and ornamenting metal that existed in Colombia at the time of the Spanish conquest.

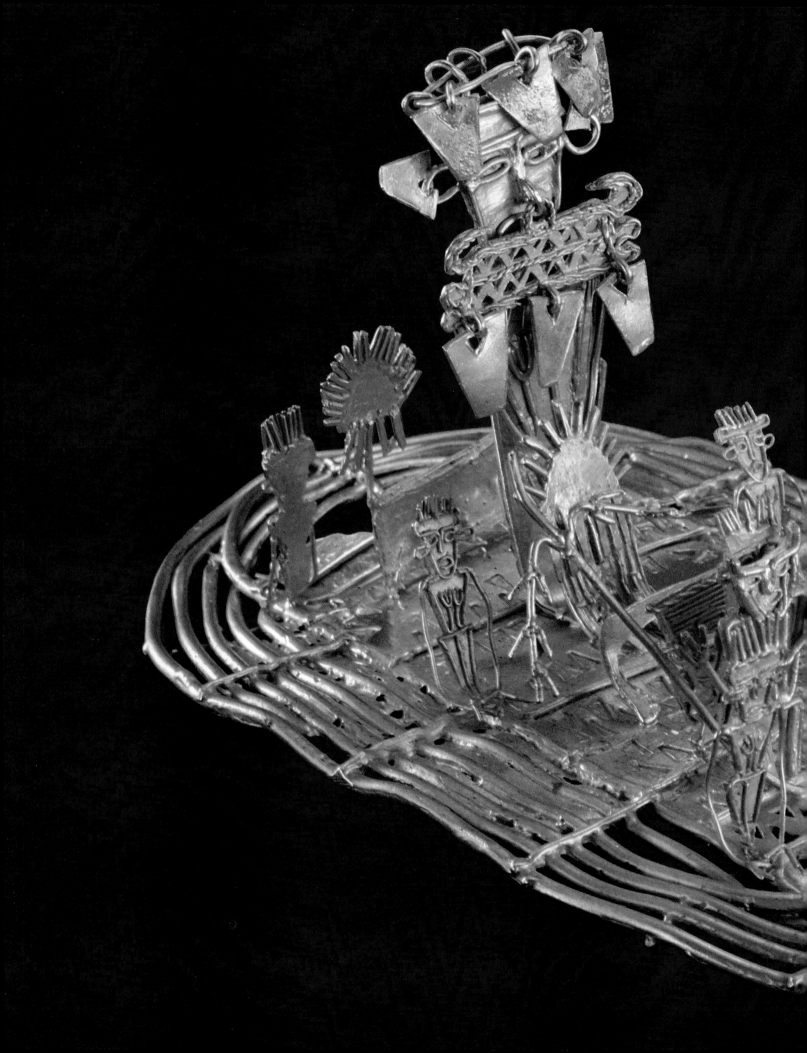

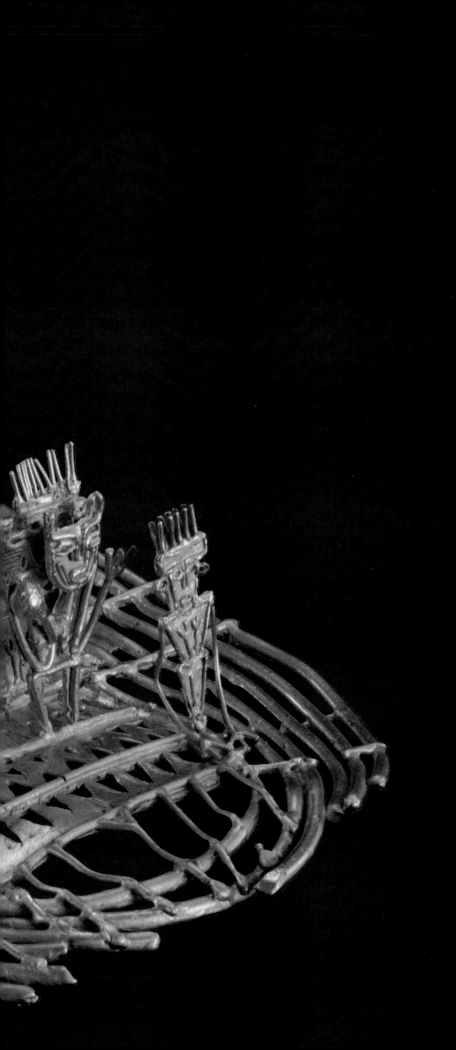

When the Spaniards and other Europeans marched through Colombia in the sixteenth century, the wealth they sought was concentrated within several extensive Indian federations and chiefdoms that traded gold widely and worked it with supreme skill. The Sinú area in the northwest, where the first explorers ventured, boasted immensely rich burial grounds and jewelry so exquisite—such as the earrings on pages 158–159—that the Sinú people were famous among other tribes for their goldwork. The Tairona, fierce highland city dwellers, executed tiny, virtuoso figure-pendants such as those on pages 165–169. They also traded actively with the people of the Muisca kingdoms, who produced their own distinctive figurines (here and pages 152–153).

Indeed, all the pieces on these pages are small, personal objects that were undoubtedly cherished as much for their artistry, shapes, and decorations as for the gold from which they were made. The form of the gold meant little to the Europeans, however. They wanted only ingots and so melted down the noseplugs, necklaces, pendants, and other ornaments seized in raids or exacted as tribute. Nor was their greed ever satisfied: the legend of El Dorado, which most likely stemmed from a Muisca ceremony and came to promise an entire realm of gold, led them to search for more than two centuries. In the end El Dorado eluded them, for it was a dream fed by the excitement of discovering a new world. The truth behind the dream is here, in what escaped the conquerors' predations.

On a golden raft attendants flank a chieftain, who is four times their size and wears an elaborate nosepiece and headdress. This extraordinary work seems to confirm the most widespread version of the El Dorado story, which told of a gilded ruler who led a ceremony on Lake Guatavita. Cast in gold, the eight-inch-long piece is a Muisca tunjo—a votive offering placed in sacred grounds and lagoons.

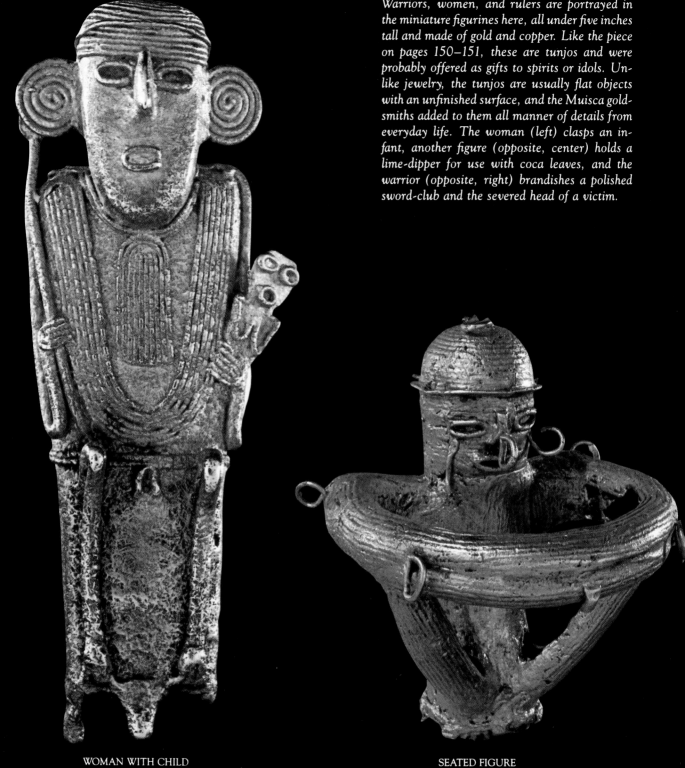

Warriors, women, and rulers are portrayed in the miniature figurines here, all under five inches tall and made of gold and copper. Like the piece on pages 150–151, these are tunjos and were probably offered as gifts to spirits or idols. Unlike jewelry, the tunjos are usually flat objects with an unfinished surface, and the Muisca goldsmiths added to them all manner of details from everyday life. The woman (left) clasps an infant, another figure (opposite, center) holds a lime-dipper for use with coca leaves, and the warrior (opposite, right) brandishes a polished sword-club and the severed head of a victim.

WOMAN WITH CHILD

SEATED FIGURE

DIGNITARY WITH NOSEPLUG   CROWNED FIGURE WITH LIME-DIPPER   WARRIOR CARRYING SEVERED HEAD

This Muisca pectoral, which has small figures at the top, is in the shape of a bird—a widespread motif in the period just before the conquest.

On the human figure of a seven-inch-high pectoral, opposite, a great diadem of golden bands and discs suggests the sun, which was at the center of Muisca religion. Fine braidwork, a large noseplug, a pair of birds at the waist, and other discs complete the ornamentation of the figure.

OVERLEAF: Six grimacing figures, four of them perched on birds' heads, are joined to the glittering pectoral above. Their wide, semicircular headdresses are similar to those on the metalwork of the Tairona, to whom the Muisca sent emeralds in return for gold nose ornaments, beads, and seashells.

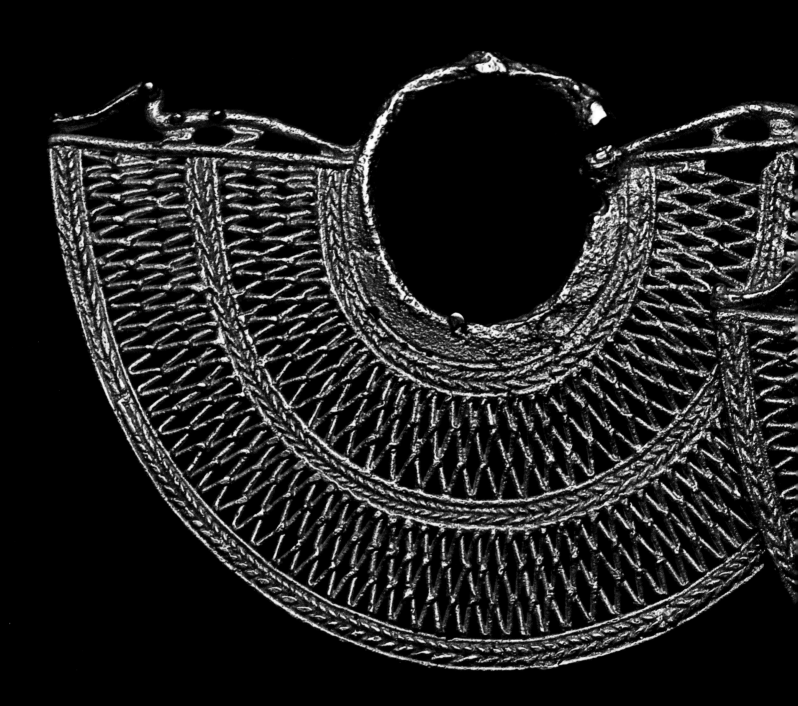

Each of these fan-shaped Sinú ear ornaments has a crocodile on either side of the loop and a delicate mesh surface that looks like filigree work. The gold, however, was not soldered—as it is in filigree—but expertly cast from a model built of wirelike threads of wax, which had been encased in a clay mold.

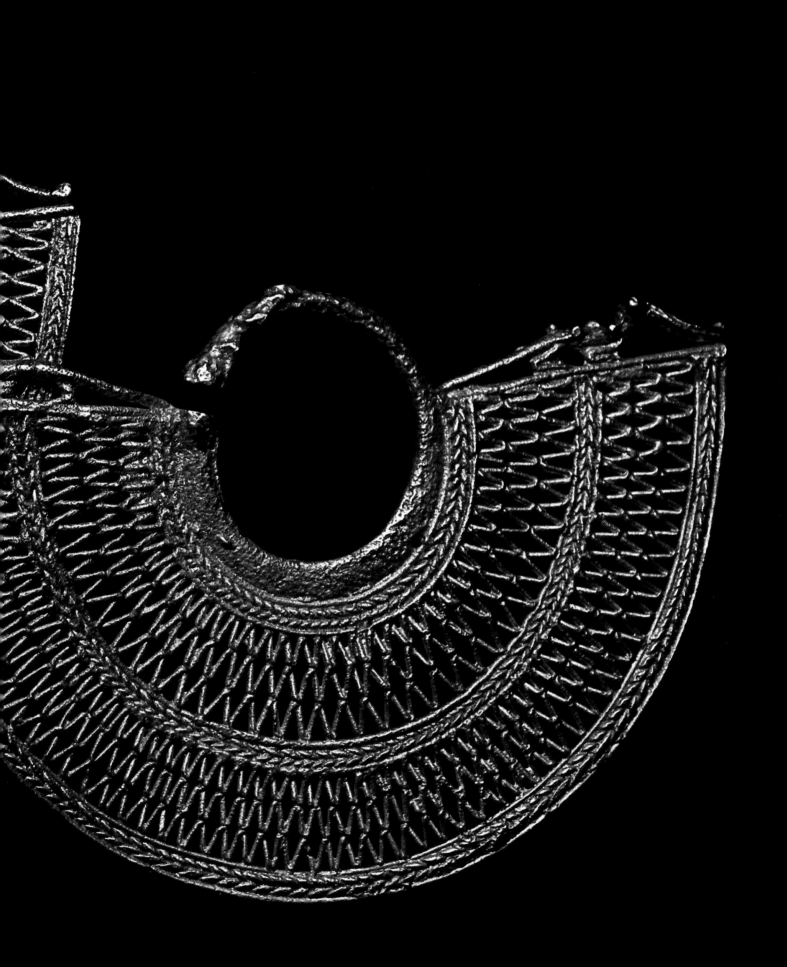

Figures cast from gold or a gold-copper alloy perch on sockets that probably capped batons or scepters of Sinú lords. On the page opposite, at top, five long-billed birds are joined to a perforated cylinder about six inches long—the largest of these staff heads. The piece just below it displays a bird with unusually thick legs but a quite lifelike beak and posture. A seated man with a nosehole that once held an ornament surmounts the third socket opposite. Directly below is a bird with rows of plumage, and next to it crouches the figure of a deer—its long face decorated with braided gold threads. The bird at right, fashioned with chest perforations, has hooks on its curved beak that once held bangles or similar tiny ornaments.

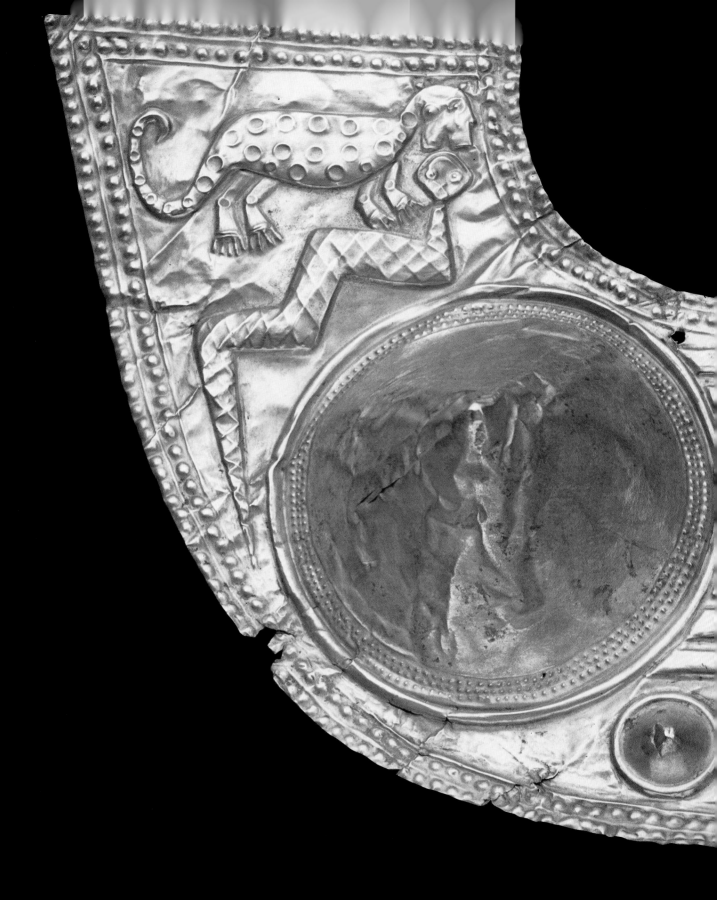

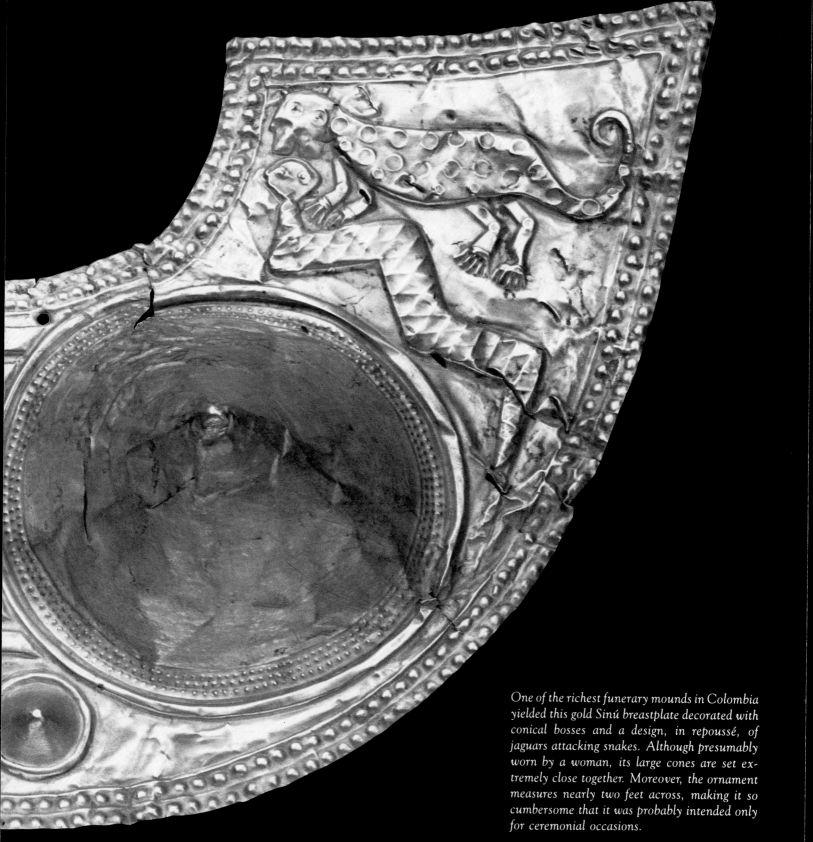

One of the richest funerary mounds in Colombia yielded this gold Sinú breastplate decorated with conical bosses and a design, in repoussé, of jaguars attacking snakes. Although presumably worn by a woman, its large cones are set extremely close together. Moreover, the ornament measures nearly two feet across, making it so cumbersome that it was probably intended only for ceremonial occasions.

In addition to a massive headdress and a complement of jewelry, the little human figure above wears a visored helmet and a pugnacious scowl. Tairona figure-pendants such as this were among the most flamboyant Colombian goldworks.

The upper half of an unusual pendant, opposite, bears the heads of two alligators, two seahorses, and at the very top, a jaguar. The lower half suggests a ceremonial knife—a rare implement in ancient Colombia. Though its provenance is unknown, the workmanship of the four-inch-high piece is thought to be Tairona, and quite possibly it was a symbol of power for a chieftain of this warlike tribe.

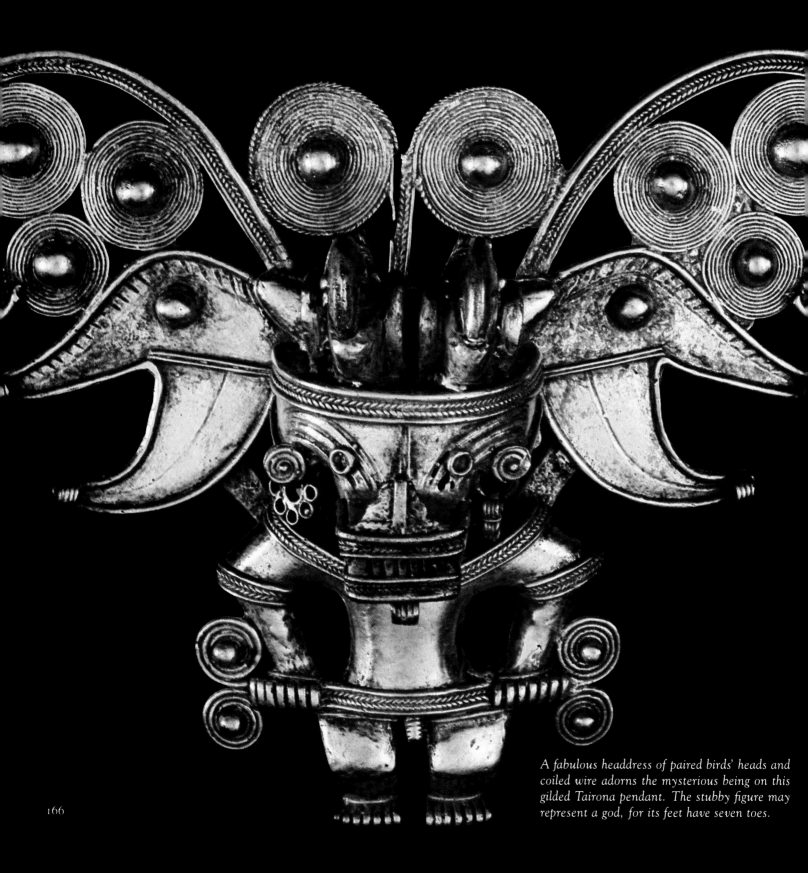

A fabulous headdress of paired birds' heads and coiled wire adorns the mysterious being on this gilded Tairona pendant. The stubby figure may represent a god, for its feet have seven toes.

Two bats hanging upside down form part of the headdress on the pendant at right, which is about three inches high. The figure may be a chieftain, typically bedecked with a noseplug, a lip plug, large earrings, and a helmet, as well as a necklace of braided gold.

OVERLEAF: *On the headdress of yet another pendant, two beasts, perhaps alligators, bare their teeth. Except for the dangling ear ornaments, this intricate piece—like the others here—was made from a single casting.*

EL DORADO: A CHRONOLOGY

PERU					
CHAVIN	PARACAS	NAZCA	MOCHE	CHIMU	INCAS

600						
500						
400						
300						
200						
100						
B.C. 0						
A.D.						
100						
200						
300						
400						
500						
600						
700						
800						
900						
1000						
1100						
1200						
1300						
1400						
1500						
1600						

The Spanish conquest of the kingdoms of gold began in the early 1500s; prior to that the chronology of South America is necessarily inexact. In Peru one of the earliest known high cultures, that of Chavín, flourished from about 600 B.C., but then by about 300 B.C. died out or was simply absorbed. Successive cultures on both the north and south coasts—the Paracas, the Nazca, the Moche, and the Chimú—rose about the time of Christ. Their lands and customs formed a heritage for the late-arriving Incas. The goldworking peoples of Colombia, who lacked the sophisticated political systems of their Peruvian neighbors, existed simultaneously—probably from dates more remote than scholars know, and far past the arrival of the Europeans.

COLOMBIA					
CALIMA	TOLIMA	QUIMBAYA	TAIRONA	MUISCA	SINU

600
500
400
300
200
100
0 B.C.
A.D.
100
200
300
400
500
600
700
800
900
1000
1100
1200
1300
1400
1500
1600

ACKNOWLEDGMENTS & CREDITS

Abbreviations:
AMNH—American Museum of Natural History, N.Y.
CG—Jim Coxe and Peter Goldberg, N.Y.
LB—Lee Boltin, Croton-on-Hudson, N.Y.
LM—Loren McIntyre, Arlington, Virginia
MAI—Museum of the American Indian, N.Y.
MMA—Metropolitan Museum of Art, N.Y.
MNA—Museo Nacional de Antropología y Arqueología, Lima
MOB—Museo de Oro, Bogotá
MOP—Museo de Oro del Peru, Lima
MRLH—Museo Rafael Larco Herrera, Lima
NYPL—New York Public Library
ROM—Royal Ontario Museum, Toronto
UP/DO—Ursula Pariser/Robert Woods Bliss Collection, Dumbarton Oaks, Washington, D.C.

We would like to thank the following for their assistance: Yoshitaro Amano, Lima; Carlos Arostegui, Department of Pre–Columbian Art, Robert Woods Bliss Collection, Dumbarton Oaks, Washington, D.C.; Elizabeth Benson, Bethesda, Maryland; Alec Bright and Dr. Luis Dugue Gomez, MOB; Richard Burger, Anthropology Department, Yale University, New Haven, Connecticut; Deanna Cross, Photographic Services, MMA; Christopher Donnan, Museum of Cultural History, University of California at Los Angeles; Fernando Dornelles and Miguel Mujica Gallo, Ambassador, Embassy of Peru, Madrid; Anne Marie Erlich, London; Dr. Alfonso Espinosa, Embassy of Peru, Washington, D.C.; David Fawcett, MAI; Miguel Mujica Gallo y Diez Canseco, MOP; Delbert Gutridge and Anne Wardwell, Cleveland Museum, Cleveland, Ohio; Dr. John Hemming, Royal Geographic Society, London; Carlos Iragorri, Avianca Airlines, N.Y.; Kathryn Jalayre, Andre Emmerich Galleries, N.Y.; Mildred Kaplan, Arte Primitivo, N.Y.; Frederick Landmann, Windsor, Vermont; Isabel Larco de Alvarez Calderon, MRLH; Loren and Sue McIntyre, Arlington, Virginia; Dr. Craig Morris, Department of Anthropology, AMNH; Juan González Navarrete, Museo de América, Madrid; Patti Nelson, St. Louis Art Museum, St. Louis, Missouri; Dr. Anne Paul, University of Georgia, Athens, Georgia; Karen Rosenbloom, Public Affairs, AMNH; Vuku Roussakis, Textile Department, AMNH; Elizabeth Routh, ROM; John Taylor, N.Y.; Luis Enrique Tord, MNA.

Maps by H. Shaw Borst
Endsheet design by Cockerell Bindery/TALAS

Cover: Harold and Erica Van Pelt, Los Angeles. 2: LB. 4–5: Michael Holford. 6: AMNH. 10: UP/DO. 12: MMA, H.B. Dick and Fletcher Funds. 13: LM, MRLH. 14(both): LM. 15: MMA, Michael C. Rockefeller Memorial Collection. 16–17: MAI. 18,19: UP/DO. 20(top): Cleveland Museum of Art, Cleveland, Ohio. 20(bottom): LB. 21: MAI. 22–23: LM. 24: Justin Kerr, N.Y. 25: LB. 26–27: St. Louis Art Museum, St. Louis, Missouri. 28–29: LM, MNA. 30: Götesburg Ethnologica Museum, Götesburg, Sweden. 31: British Museum, Museum of Mankind, London. 32, 33: AMNH. 34: CG. 35–38: AMNH. 40(both): LM, MNA. 41: LB. 42–43: LM, MNA. 44–45: Götesburg Ethnologica Museum, Götesburg, Sweden. 46–47: ROM. 48, 49: Linden Museum, Stuttgart. 50: MMA, Michael C. Rockefeller Memorial Collection. 51: LM, MOP. 52–53: LM, Amano Museum, Lima. 54(left): Andre Emmerich, N.Y. 54(right), 55: LM, MRLH. 56(top): LM, Amano Museum, Lima. 56(bottom): LB. 56(right): LM, MRLH. 57: Justin Kerr, N.Y. 58: Museum für Völkerkunde, Munich. 59: Masakatsu Yamanoto, Tokyo. 60–61 (both): LB, MMA. 62–63: LM, MOP. 64–65: MMA. 66–67: Oronoz. 68–69: LB. 70–71: MMA, Gift of Alice K. Bache. 72–73: AMNH, Collection of Frederick Landemann. 75: Thomas Gilcrease Institute of American History and Art, Tulsa, Oklahoma. 76,77: NYPL. 78–79: ROM. 79: NYPL. 80: Colour Library International. 81: Alan Becker/Photo Researchers. 82: LM. 83(top): George Holton/Photo Researchers. 83(bottom): George Holton/Photo Researchers. 84–85: LM. 86, 87: NYPL. 88, 89: Rare Books Division, NYPL. 90: LM. 91: CG. 92–93: Oronoz. 94–95: LM, MRLH. 96: Oronoz. 97: ROM. 98–99: LM, MOP. 100–101: Oronoz. 102(top): LM, MOP. 102(bottom): LB. 103(left): LB. 103(right): CG. 104(left): MMA, Bequest of Alice K. Bache. 104(center): ROM. 104(right): Oronoz. 105(left): ROM. 105(center): CG. 105(right): LB. 106–107: Oronoz. 108–109: Musée de l'Homme, Paris. 110–113: Rare Books Division, NYPL. 114–115: George Holton/Photo Researchers. 116–117: LM. 118: George Gerster/Photo Researchers. 119: George Holton/Photo Researchers. 120–121: MAI. 123: LB. 124, 125: LM, MOB. 126–127: British Museum, Museum of Mankind, London. 127: MMA, Bequest of Alice K. Bache. 128: LM, MOB. 129: Victor Englebert/Susan Griggs Agency. 130–131(all): LM, MOB. 132, 133: British Museum, Museum of Mankind, London. 134: LB. 135 (left): Jean Mazenod, Paris. 135(right): LB. 136: British Museum, Museum of Mankind, London. 137: Victor Englebert/Susan Griggs Agency. 138–139: LM, MOB. 140–141: Christian Lemzaoud/Musée de l'Homme, Paris. 142: British Library, London. 143: Oronoz. 144–145: British Library, London. 146–147: Rare Books Division, NYPL. 149: LM, MOB. 150–151: LB. 152–153(all): LM, MOB. 154: LB. 155, 156–157: Andre Emmerich, N.Y. 158–159: LM, MOB. 160(top): CG, MAI. 160(left): UP/DO. 160(right): LM, MOB. 161(left and right): UP/DO. 161(top): LM, MOB. 162–163: LB. 164: AMNH. 165: UP/DO. 166–167: LM, MOB. 167: Andre Emmerich, N.Y. 168–169: MMA, H.G. Bache Fund.

SUGGESTED READINGS

Benson, Elizabeth P., *The Mochica, A Culture of Peru.* Praeger Publishers, 1972.

Bray, Warwick, *The Gold of El Dorado.* Times Newspapers, Ltd., 1978.

Donnan, Christopher B., *Moche Art and Iconography.* UCLA Latin American Center Publications, 1976.

Emmerich, André, *Sweat of the Sun and Tears of the Moon, Gold and Silver in Pre-Columbian Art.* Hacker Art Books, 1977.

Hemming, John, *The Conquest of the Incas.* Harcourt, Brace, Jovanovich, Inc., 1973.

———, *The Search For El Dorado.* E.P. Dutton, 1979.

Jones, Julie and Warwick Bray, *El Dorado: The Gold of Ancient Colombia.* Center for Inter-American Relations, 1974.

Kubler, George, *The Art and Architecture of Ancient America.* Penguin Books, Inc., 1970.

Lapiner, Alan, *Pre-Columbian Art of South America.* Harry N. Abrams, Inc., 1976.

Lothrop, Samuel K., *Treasures of Ancient America: Columbian Art from Mexico to Peru.* Rizzoli International Publications, Inc., 1979.

Mason, Alden J., *The Ancient Civilizations of Peru.* Penguin Books, Inc., 1957.

Parsons, Lee A., *Pre-Columbian Art.* Harper & Row Publishers, Inc., 1980.

Reichel-Dolmatoff, Gerardo, *San Agustín: A Culture of Colombia.* Praeger Publishers, 1972.

INDEX

Page numbers in **boldface type** refer to illustrations and captions.